CRICKET
~ WITH ~
GRACE

AN ILLUSTRATED
ANTHOLOGY ON 'W.G.'

Compiled by

David Rayvern Allen

UNWIN

HYMAN

LONDON SYDNEY WELLINGTON

UNWIN HYMAN LIMITED
15–17 Broadwick Street
London W1V 1FP

Allen & Unwin Australia Pty Ltd
8 Napier Street,
North Sydney,
NSW 2060,
Australia

Allen & Unwin New Zealand Pty Ltd with the Port Nicholson Press
Press Compusales Building, 75 Ghuznee Street, Wellington,
New Zealand

British Library Cataloguing in Publication Data
Allen, David Rayvern
Cricket with Grace: an illustrated anthology of W. G.
1. Cricket. Grace, W. G. (William Gilbert), 1848–1915
I. Title
796.3580924
ISBN 0–04–440478–6

Designed by Paul Saunders

Typeset by Wyvern Typesetting Ltd., Bristol

Printed in Great Britain by Butler and Tanner Ltd., Frome

CONTENTS

Acknowledgements

I would like to record my gratitude to the following who have helped in various ways during the assembly of this book: Bill Neill-Hall; Helen Wythers; Merlin Unwin; Stephen Green; Derek Lodge; Nicholas Potter; John Bright-Holmes; 'Bunty' Ireland; and the staff of the BBC Reference Library, the Marylebone Library and Cambridge University Library.

A special vote of thanks is due to Jenny and Roger Mann, not only for some excellent hospitality, but also for affording access to their wide-ranging collection of cricketana.

I would also like to thank the following for permission to reproduce material: Mrs Rowbottom, 'My "W. G."' by A. E. Lawton; Stephen Green, 'A Transfer of Allegiance'; Philip Bailey, 'W. G. Story'; Phoenix House, *W. G. Grace, Cricketing Lives* by Clifford Bax; Unwin Hyman, *W. G. Grace, The Great Cricketer* by A. A. Thomson; Chapman & Hall, *Reminiscences of a Vintner* by Ian Maxwell; the *Manchester Guardian*, 'A Day of Grace' by George Marvill; E. W. Swanton, 'Closing of an Epoch'; Eyre & Spottiswode, *The Age of Grace 1864–1894* by Roland Bowen.

Every effort has been made to trace the copyright holders of the material reprinted in this anthology. The author and the publishers would be glad to hear from any copyright holders they have not been able to contact.

Since a large number of the illustrations were taken when the science of photography was still in its infancy, unfortunately many of them are lacking in quality. However, due to their historical significance they have been included despite their technical shortcomings.

Rider to Statistical Survey see pages 152 to 160
In 1973, G. Neville Weston issued 'W. G. Grace, the Great Cricketer, a statistical record of his performances in Minor Cricket'. Between that year and 1979, there were produced typescript corrections and additions, and first, second, third and fourth supplements in limited editions. In 1980, a final supplement was issued (described as first) from which was extracted the above summary. In the Preface to this supplement Weston notes 'there may yet be more runs and wickets to be found but as I have now reached the magic figure of 100,000 for W.G.'s runs in *all* kinds of cricket . . . ' Weston based his remark on a figure of 54,904 for W.G. in *first-class* matches, in conjunction with his own *minor* match total.

The Association of Cricket Statisticians, and Philip Bailey in particular regard to Grace, have thrown considerable light on the grading of fixtures and, as is seen, their estimate of W.G.'s first-class runs is somewhat lower. In conjuction with Weston's minor match total it would leave Grace still wanting the magic six figures. However, redistributing the riches should not necessarily alter the overall sum. We can rest assured the Great Man scored in excess of 100,000 runs in all cricket.

Foreword

For one who would write a Foreword, this book raises the problem of an unusual amalgam. The compiler, David Rayvern Allen, is not only a close friend but has much the same outlook as the writer of this piece. His subject, however, William Gilbert Grace, is for our generations an almost legendary figure, remote in many ways but familiar as a fairy tale.

Grace was, though some may argue to the contrary, an eminent Victorian, a highly gifted cricketer and a quite strikingly remarkable human being. In his own time, and even more to the succeeding generations, he seemed quite unreal, displaying in some ways, an almost magical personality, in others a crude earthy character. He possessed abnormal skill at a game not merely of his choice but one which he virtually created.

In forming this anthology, Mr Allen has not cast aside the element of legend in this most unusual man but has gone to great pains to observe the realities behind the legend. The result is a fascinating study, not only of a person and not only of a game, but of a passage of English life. The compiler's pleasure in building this picture is effected in the result. He has used the material to make a fresh-seeming composition which is also fun.

John Arlott

INTRODUCTION

'LET us say Grace!' Even the most uncompromising religious zealot might allow the mind to wander from the immediate thanksgiving to that of a figure who was part of the fabric of late Victorian England. The name Grace, exhibited proudly by an existing store in midtown Manhattan and also portrayed as a fictional fraternal concern in a recent television sit-com, can bring but one mental association for the true Anglophile. Accompanying the thought is a sense of history and wonderment.

A century after his pomp, why does Grace still generate so much interest? Why are his exploits recounted with such relish? Why does his name occur more than any other single player in the 10,000 or so books on cricket? More significantly, why does his name appear more than any other cricketer's in books that are not about cricket?

For would-be interrogators, the answers to these and further pertinent questions are to be found in the pages that follow. Some queries remain to be answered and perhaps never will be. Exhaustive though the treatment of Grace has been there are facets of his life, particularly with regard to his domestic arrangements and inner thoughts, that are a closed book.

So, of what does this anthology comprise? The aim has been, as far as is possible, to build a framework that relates, however tenuously, to the chronology of Grace's career. There is a cross-mix of contemporary comment and preteritive view, some of it is adulatory, some of it pragmatic. There is also balanced account and humorous anecdote, often contradictory and a few of the latter, no doubt, apocryphal. We have to accept that Simon Pure may live only in the eyes of the beholder and that 'one of the most valuable features of journalism is that it realizes that truth is not a solid but a fluid'. It is as well to mention, too, that even with the treasure-house of tales surrounding Grace a degree of repetition is unavoidable – writers tend to plunder the best that is available.

Contained within are a résumé of Grace's career by Arthur Waring; face-to-face interviews in *Strand Magazine* and *The Captain*; appreciations by Horace G. Hutchinson, Major C. H. B. Pridham and Neville Cardus; recollections from fellow doctor-cricketer Arthur Conan Doyle and the 'demon' bowler F. R. Spofforth; a literary working relationship described by Arthur Porritt; ruminatory radio talks from one-time England captains Archie MacLaren and 'Plum' Warner; an unpublished composition, with a foreword from Jack Hobbs, by A. E. Lawton who skippered Derbyshire during the early 1900s; imaginative examples of a confluence of fanciful characterization with factual overtones; assessments of the man in the context of his time by a school of distinguished scribes, including E. W. 'Jim' Swanton and Roland Bowen; opinions concerning the rift with Gloucestershire and stories of the days with London County; period berhymes; obituary articles; statistical summaries and all of it interwoven with yarn upon yarn. And this is far from the whole: the contents pages reveal the full listings.

Sir (John Randolph) Shane Leslie has defined unique individuals like Grace, who set yardsticks seemingly beyond the reach of mere mortals, as 'part of the national baggage'. Let us now travel with him . . .

'The King of Cricket'

by Albert Craig 'The Surrey Poet'

HE would scorn to ask a favour
  From his host of friendly foes,
If there's anything worth knowing
  In the game, the veteran knows.
His eye retains its lustre,
  His judgment's sound and true,
Tho' he cannot run the notches
  With the pace he used to do.
Still, he's the undisputed knack
  Of knocking up a score,
He buckle's on his armour still,
  Altho' he's fifty-four.

We saw and gloried in his skill
  When some of us were young,
We revelled in his doughty deeds,
  Proudly his praises sung.
His 'off-drives' captivated us,
  His lovely 'cuts' for four
Enchanted those who witness'd them,
  And raised a mighty roar.
'Tis nigh on forty years ago,
  Those days are past and gone.
And yet our monarch of the game
  Has still the armour on.

He plays the dear old summer game
  As cricket should be played,
In all his actions dignified,
  Still calm and undismayed.
It is as famous Hayward says:
  'The man would be a "bold un"
Who fancied he'd a wrinkle
  That he could give the "old un." '
The little Surrey Marvel
  Would tell you to his face
That England is not England
  Minus our Champion, Grace.

— 1 —

EARLY GAMES

Starting Off

FREDERICK G. WARNE

WILLIAM GILBERT GRACE was born on July 18th, 1848, at Downend, a small village near Bristol, situate in the county of Gloucestershire. His father was Dr. Henry Mills Grace, who was quite an enthusiast in the matter of cricket, and both in his student days and in after-life, when he had the exacting duties of a country medical practice upon him, lost no oppor- tunity of playing and watching his beloved game, and instilling into his children a like passion. Of his five sons, all became medicos, and all votaries of the bat and ball! Dr. Henry Mills Grace settled at Downend in 1831. His wife was Martha Pocock, daughter of Mr. George Pocock, who owned a private boarding school at St. Michael's Hill, Bristol. . . .

In the days when W.G.'s father waxed earnest and enthusiastic over cricket, the facilities for its enjoyment were not so full as they are to-day by a very long way. Clubs were few in number; grounds were fewer still. 'When,' says W.G., 'my father became a medical student, it was impossible for him to get away during the afternoon or evening, as most students do in the present day, and if he had not resorted to extraordi- nary hours he would have been compelled to give up playing. Two to three days a week throughout the cricket season, he and a number of his companions were in the habit of going to the Downs (Clifton) and practising between the hours of five and eight in the morning. In that way only could he continue the game he loved so well; and I remember we tried to follow in his footsteps in after years, at not quite so early an hour. He had the great qualities of perseverance and concentration, and he diligently impressed upon us the need for cultivating them.'

To encourage his boys in the game, the worthy Doctor had a

somewhat rough-and-ready cricket-pitch laid in front of his house, and out of this there grew a club which was afterwards to achieve some local fame – the Mangotsfield. The people around became more or less infected with the Doctor's love of the pastime, and to keep pace with their growing enthusiasm the Mangotsfield Club was started. When the Doctor's family increased, Downend House, where he had hitherto resided, became too straitened in accommodation, and removal was effected to another house in the same village – 'The Chestnuts'. Here the beloved game was pursued with perhaps even greater vigour than before. 'W.G.' was only about two years old when he made the acquaintance of 'The Chestnuts' as an abode, so that his cricket education had not as yet begun; but one can imagine him even then taking an interest in the game, watching his father and uncle and elder brothers, 'launching a ball at three sorts of bars stuck in the earth, on which is placed transversely a bar of less importance' – as a Frenchman described the game of cricket many years afterwards, when W.G.'s fame had travelled to Paris. The cricket-pitch was located in the orchard of 'The Chestnuts', denuded of some of its fruit-trees for the purpose; and here W.G., when he arrived at such age that he could be duly entrusted with a bat, was initiated into the rudiments of the game under the painstaking instruction of Uncle Pocock – Mr. Alfred Pocock, as we should call him – another cricket enthusiast of the family. Certain times were set apart for cricket practice in the orchard, the elder members of the family being allowed the privilege of a quarter-of-an-hour's batting each, and the younger ones five minutes. To make up the deficiency the youngsters would steal many a quiet practice at other times, with the aid of 'boots' as bowler, and the dogs of the house as fielders! 'From first to last,' Mr. Grace says in his capital autobiography, 'we had three dogs, whose services were invaluable: Don, Ponto, and Noble. Noble was a most intelligent retriever, and would go into the water for the ball without hesitation. Ponto took his position at the side of the bowler, and watched the flight of the ball with as much care as the batsman; and when it was hit over the trees would listen carefully until he heard it crash among the branches, and then make straight to the spot where it fell. His instinct was remarkable, and with a little training we got him to do wonders. A ball bowled to the off, he expected to be hit on that side. They had plenty of pluck, too; for they would present their chest to the ball, no matter how hard it was hit, and time after time I have seen them catch it on the bound with their mouth.' . . .

Under Uncle Pocock's methodical tuition, W.G. made great headway towards style and correctness in playing. Indeed, it is asserted that at the age of nine his play was as correct as at twenty, and distinguished by his wonderful straight defence and placing, which in later years have won the enthusiastic admiration of all who have witnessed it. 'I should like to be able to say,' Mr. Grace writes, 'that I had no difficulty in learning cricket, and that proficiency came to me much easier than it comes to other boys. The reverse is the truth. I had to work as hard at learning cricket as I ever worked at my profession, or anything else. Very quickly I learned that there was no royal road there, and that if I wanted to be a good cricketer, I must persevere. I was fortunate in having a good tutor, and a strong gift of perseverance; that is as much as I can say to students of the game.'

W.G.'s very earliest memories are of cricket. He has, it is said, a recollection of seeing a match played at Bristol between the All England eleven and twenty-two of West Gloucestershire, when a little lad of six years of age, seated upon his father's knee, on which occasion two or three of the elder players wore top hats! . . . The first match in which he played – West Gloucestershire v. Bedminster – took place in 1857, when his score was 3, not out. He was then nine years of age. He played two other games for West Gloucestershire that year, but only made one more run. In 1858, he played six innings for 4 runs; 1859, nine innings for 12 runs; 1860, four innings for 82 runs; 1861, ten innings for 46 runs; 1862, five innings for 53 runs; and in 1863, nineteen innings for 350 runs, six times not out. In the following year – he was sixteen now – W.G.'s first great performance took place, when in a match at Brighton between the Gentlemen of South Wales and the Gentlemen of Sussex he made 170 and 56 not out, and took two wickets in the first innings! His score was the highest for his side in each innings, and the bat which he was given as a memento of the event he retains to this day. It bears the following inscription: 'Presented by Mr. John Lloyd, secretary of the South Wales Cricket Club, to Mr. W. G. Grace on the occasion of his making 170 runs without giving a chance, and 56 not out when playing for that club v. the Gentlemen of the County of Sussex, on July 14th, 15th, and 16th, 1864, at the Hove Ground, Brighton.' . . .

W.G.'s early education was received at the village school; thence he went to a school at Winterbourne, Glos. and later he was placed with Mr. Malpass, of Rudgway House School. At the last-named, Mr. Methven Brownlee tells us, he 'earned the reputation of being a steady working lad, accurate in mathematics, with no mischief in him, passionately fond of collecting birds' eggs and snakes, which caused rather a division of feeling at "The Chesnuts". The snakes were the terror of his mother and sisters, and had to be smuggled into the house and hidden in secret corners. Now and then one popped out at an inconvenient moment, and W.G. had to listen to the screaming of his sisters, usually followed by a paternal lecture and dire prophecies of what the end of such tastes would be.'

In the year 1863, the West Gloucestershire Club (which was really our old friend, the Mangotsfield Club, under a more high-sounding designation) had regularly playing for it the following members of the Grace family – E. M., Henry, Alfred, Fred, W. G. and Uncle Pocock. One story which W.G. tells concerning the West Gloucestershire is too good to be lost. It was the occasion of a match with Redland in 1858. All the members of the family, excepting Fred, were to play, and they were on the ground betimes. But alas! one on-looker, who had been drinking rather freely, had elected to lie at full-length unpleasantly close to the wicket, and persuasion proved useless in inducing him to move. What followed may be given in W.G.'s own words: 'When the Redland eleven arrived, an attempt was made to clear the ground, but our noisy critic resented, and my father, much against his will, had to resort to force of arms. Calling up my brother, Alfred, who had a fair reputation as a boxer, he ordered him to remove the obstinate individual; he did not seem to object, and the unusual sight of a fight *before* a cricket-match was witnessed. Two minutes proved that Alfred had a very easy undertaking, and he dealt very lightly with his opponent, who had the sense, or feeling, to cry, "Enough," and left the field altogether. The little preliminary excitement added to the interest of the match, and a keen and enjoyable one it became. Redland scored 51 first innings; 116 second. West Gloucestershire scored 67 first, and were 84 in the second for five wickets, with about an hour remaining to play, when our friend of the morning turned up again.

'This time he brought his friends with him, who asserted that he had been unfairly treated. It seemed absurd that a cricket match should be delayed a second time for so small a matter; but there was no alternative. Alfred had a tougher task this time; but, rising to the occasion, he polished off his opponent in an artistic and satisfactory manner. That did not satisfy him or his friends; for they betook themselves to a convenient heap of stones, and a free fight ensued. For a little while the West Gloucestershire and Redland, fighting side by side, had rather the worst of the contest; but charging shoulder to shoulder with stumps and bats, they drove the crowd from the heap of stones, and assumed the offensive. A lively state of affairs prevailed the next half-hour. In the meantime my father had ridden off hurriedly to the nearest magistrate, who returned with him, and threatened to read the Riot Act if they did not disperse. Fortunately, for the reputation of the two clubs and villagers, so extreme a measure was unnecessary, and the opposition collapsed, but the match had to be abandoned.'

DR W. G. GRACE: THE KING OF CRICKET, *H. A. Burleigh, 1899*

— 2 —

ON FOREIGN SOIL

Grace in Canada

CLIFFORD BAX

THEY sailed from Liverpool on August the 8th, amused themselves with shovel-board, peg-ringing, chair-jumping and whist, and arrived at Port Levi, in Quebec, on the 17th. On the 22nd they played their first match, against 'Twenty-two of Montreal'. A local paper gives us an interesting snapshot of W.G. when he was twenty-four. 'W. Grace', the reporter wrote, 'is a large-framed loose-jointed man, and you would say that his gait was a trifle peculiar, but when he goes into the field you see that he is quick-sighted, sure-handed and light-footed as the rest. He always goes in first, and to see him tap the ball gently to the off for one, draw it to the on for two, pound it to the limits for four, drive it heaven knows where for six, looks as easy as rolling off a log.' In this game the sixer landed in a field of melons and in consequence took long to retrieve.

In Canada the young Englishmen found somewhat elementary opposition. W.G. amassed a huge collection of easy runs and then, spurred by the success of a lob-bowler in the team, decided to prove that he also could mop up Canadian wickets. Of course there were many banquets, and I do not know why Grace, rather than the Skipper, should have been required to 'speak' on these occasions. Nobody will suppose that Grace was a brilliant orator, for 'omnia non possumus omnes'. He realized that he was just the ordinary ineloquent Englishman, though not exactly the 'strong, silent man' of Edwardian fiction, and guessing that his prowess might involve him in speech-making he cunningly devised a formula.

At Montreal he had to reply to the toast of 'The Champion Batsman of

Cricketdom'. 'Gentlemen,' he said, 'I beg to thank you for the honour you have done me. I never saw better bowling than I have seen today, and I hope to see as good wherever I go.' At Ottawa he said, 'Gentlemen, I thank you for the honour you have done me. I never saw a better ground than I have seen today, and I hope to see as good wherever I go.' At Toronto he said, 'I never saw such good fellows as I have seen today, and I hope to see as good wherever I go.' At 'London' he and the skipper of the side defeated two ladies in a game of croquet, an incident which enabled him to say at the subsequent banquet, 'Ladies and Gentlemen, I thank you for the honour you have done me. I never saw prettier ladies than I have seen today, and I hope . . .' etc. At the end of the short tour W.G. varied his speech by saying, 'I never saw better oysters than I have seen today and I hope . . .' etc. We realize that he had a sense of humour when we learn that years afterwards he once asked, 'Shall I make one of my Canadian speeches?'

W. G. GRACE, CRICKETING LIVES, Phoenix House, 1952

Grace in Australia

ERIC MIDWINTER

THE first overseas tour from England had been to North America, when, in 1859, a twelve-strong professional squad had endured appalling Atlantic crossings and almost as dreadful playing conditions (they fielded in great-coats at Hamilton in several inches of snow) to thrash five teams overwhelmingly. But it was the more 'English' and less cosmopolitan Australia, which was to dominate the overseas cricket scene. The Melbourne Cricket Club was formed in 1838 and the first inter-colonial match, resulting in a narrow defeat for Victoria at the hands of New South Wales, took place at the height of the gold rush in 1856.

Grace's first tour of 1873 had been preceded by two other trips. Two caterers, Felix Spiers and Christopher Ponds, who were busily making fortunes providing refreshments for the gold-miners, were responsible for the first. On Christmas Eve 1861, H. H. Stephenson and eleven fellow-professionals, mainly from Surrey, disembarked at Melbourne. Ten thousand Australians greeted them, and fifteen thousand watched their opening fixture on Melbourne's spacious ground with its magnificent pavilion and impressive grandstands, the first major cricket ground of the modern era. Each player wore a sash and a ribbon on his featherweight sun helmet, the colour corresponding to the key on the programme for ease of identification. The professionals earned £150 plus expenses, and Pond and Spiers made over £11,000 profit from the twelve-match tour.

Two years later, in 1863, George Parr (who, like one or two other northern 'pros', has jibbed at the 1861 voyage after the horrors of the American crossing) was persuaded, by Stephenson's triumph, by a first-class passage and a guarantee of £250, to lead a formidable combination to Australia. This was the tour E. M. Grace had joined and about which he wrote at the time in great detail and with an acute eye for Australia's 'bounceable' character. He spoke of the unique openings for venturesome enterprise, and also of how 'cricket reigned supreme' because 'everything which keeps them united to Britain and to Britain's green and to Britain's people, everything which binds them in any way close to those they left behind, is regarded with feelings of no ordinary pleasure'. Although XXII of New South Wales ran them extremely close, Parr's side survived the tour unbeaten. Charles Lawrence had, after the 1861/2 trip, remained behind as a coach, and, at the end of the 1863/4 tour, William Caffyn, who had been a stalwart on all three overseas programmes, began seven years' sterling work as a coach, mainly with the Melbourne Club. Some commentators claim that his influence more than anyone's was responsible for the rapid improvement in Australian cricket. An unaccountable time passed. Charles Lawrence brought over to England his aboriginal cricketers who doubled as boomerang-throwers, in 1868, to the confusion of some Englishmen, who formed very strange views of Australian life and cricket. But it was not until the winter of 1873 that another English party set forth to Australia.

W. G. Grace had visited Canada and the USA the year before for a relaxing tour, despite suffering the foulest of seasickness aboard the SS *Sarmation* on the outward and the SS *Prussian* on the inward journey. The games were easy, and W.G. contributed 540 of the 1,666 runs scored by the Englishmen. They had been invited by a Toronto businessman, Mr Pottieson, and the trip was organized by Fitzgerald, the secretary of MCC . . . In Australia the standard of play and the tenacity of the players was much higher, however, than in the US and Canada. It was Melbourne Cricket Club which had, in the spring of 1873, issued the invitation, and it was W. G. Grace who organized the response. He groaned that he was 'heartweary' at his efforts to raise a side, but his niggardly terms – second-class passage and a miserly £170 fee – scarcely helped. Some professionals were offended and refused, leaving the party weakened by the absence of Emmett and Shaw among several others. However, James Lillywhite and Southerton (who was to take no less than 320 wickets) joined with the Gloucester amateurs, Fred Grace, Bush and W. R. Gilbert in a mainly south of England group, and off they sailed in October.

The success of the tour was heavily dependent on W.G., to say the least. He was allowed very generous expenses and a prolonged gratis honeymoon, courtesy of the Melbourne Cricket Club, was an extra-ordinary perquisite. But he had to play in every match, and, if a match finished early, he had to provide exhibition cricket. Maybe the inter-lock of Grace the drawcard and Grace the wage-earner fed the rumour that he had backed himself not to be bowled out on Australian soil. When in the opening match against Victoria, Harry Boyle clean bowled him, there was wild excitement. (F. R. Spofforth, incidentally, first came into prominence during this tour, when he bowled W.G. in the nets.) Assuredly there was betting involved in the cricket, all of which stimulated further interest, as it had done in earlier times in England and the telegraph was used to transmit scores for the very first time.

It is as well to stress the commercial character of these tours. This is not done cynically: as far as one can judge (and in spite of the fudging of the professional–amateur boundary) the enterprises were honestly, even courageously organized. There was probably some thought of spreading the gospel and bringing the faith to the primitives, but this was a secondary consideration. What it was not was international cricket. The English sides were not recognized as representative of the nation, and Australia was not yet regarded as a nation. The rivalry was there: it was personal and it was, increasingly, Englishman versus Australian. But it was not England versus Australia.

No one would deny that this was a most arduous venture. W. G. Grace, in rotund Victorian phrases, described some of the rigours in his memoirs. To begin with, the sea journey in 1873 took over seven weeks, on the *Mirzapare* to Ceylon and thence by the *Nabia*. Including the return journey, this meant fifteen weeks – nearly a third of the year – at sea, plenty of time for W.G. to indulge his devotion to whist. Then consider the following: the tourists had to travel from Ballarat to Stowell, a distance of seventy-four miles, over rough bush track. They travelled in a Cobb's coach, little more than an open cart, in pitiless heat through thick dust. Within minutes, they were 'up to the hocks' in choking white dust. The journey began at 8.30 am and it was 8.30 in the evening before Stowell was reached. The game began the following day on a field ploughed only three months earlier and upon which grass seed had been sown in honour of the English cricketers' visit. The match completed, despite a plague of flies, the tourists rose the following morning at 4.30 am and set off for Warrnambool. The first leg of this jaunt took them to Ararat, a journey of ninety-one miles. They may have conjectured wryly about Noah's connections with the original Ararat, for this trip was negotiated through torrential rain, with the sportsmen soaked utterly to the skin. The Cobb's coach found the mud of the Ararat track as impenetrable as the dust of the Stowell road, and it took twelve hours – not much more than seven miles an hour – to reach Ararat. After the briefest of respites, the remainder of the journey to Warrnambool was undertaken. This was thirty miles, again in atrociously muddy conditions, and over five hours elapsed before their destination was sighted, an average rate of six miles an hour. It was well-nigh midnight when the exhausted and half-drowned party arrived in Warrnambool, having spent nineteen hours on the road. Next day they had to be ready for cricket.

That was a difficult but not wholly unrepresentative week for W.G. and his compatriots. It must have been a test of the strongest of constitutions and it reads not unlike the narrative of some epic military exercise in one or other of Britain's African colonies. Opponents in such places as Stowell and Warrnambool were by no means top class and the Englishmen were constantly frustrated by bad pitches. According to Grace, a bushel of pebbles had to be collected from a wicket in Tasmania before play commenced.

Grace's party overcame these handicaps royally. They won twelve of the fifteen matches – all against odds – losing three, and W.G. had a batting average of 39 (758 runs) and took 65 wickets (average 7.4); his brother Fred was second in both bowling and batting. Perhaps the proudest performance was the defeat of a strong joint Victoria/New South Wales XV by 218 runs, while the Champion's own best feat was 126 against XVIII of Victoria. The crowds were phenomenal: 15,000 had turned up for the Victoria match, and 20,000 watched the English play the Ballarat XXII. The enthusiasm of the welcome was equally magnificent. Torchlight processions, troupes of dashing horsemen, mayoral receptions and stirring military bands were deployed to enliven their welcome, while the private hospitality was no less opulent. Grace recorded that he hunted rabbits, pigeons, kangaroo, quail, plover and goldfish, the last of which he ate and found 'very good, too'. The young Mrs. Grace stayed with friends in the large cities while her untiring spouse stopped cricket only to start shooting, driving on bush tracks and tossing on coastal steamers in a ceaseless cycle of frenetic activity. It is typical of Grace – perhaps of the Victorian bourgeois male – that his honeymoon did not encapsulate that brief phase of private passion and constant attention of the romantic definition.

The Australians were unstinting in their praise for W.G. – 'a freak of nature, a cricket phenomenon' said the Melbourne press. Nonetheless, there was considerable irritation and argument, and, indeed, that strange compound of affection and abrasiveness which has long characterized England/Australia cricket began at this juncture. Grace was not blameless. He was loud and contemptuous in his criticisms of pitches, although his brother Edward must have forewarned him. More justifiably, he took grave exception to the Australian practice of moving from a rough to a smooth pitch for the home team's innings. He was equally severe on umpires, growing all but choleric at those officiating when XXII of Castlemaine were the opposition. There was much talk of Australians failing to abide by umpiring decisions, and much of the antagonism was apparently personalized between Grace and the Australian cricketer and administrator, John Conway.

The Australians were much less genial than in the 1860s, improved standards and heightened aspirations having sharpened their game. They found Grace overbearing and petty, and they evidently judged him an ingrate apropos the hospitality urged upon him and the money that he was coining. One Australian newspaper summed it up at the end of the tour: 'Now it must be confessed, if only in a shamefaced fashion, that in Australia we did not take too kindly to W.G. For so big a man he is surprisingly tenacious on very small points. We duly admired him at the wicket, but thought him too apt to wrangle in the spirit of a duo-decimo attorney over small points of the game.' Fred Grace, the gentlest of the brothers but as fiercely loyal to the family name as any of them, was perhaps more sensitive to the atmosphere: 'We were met', he said dolefully in *Lillywhite's* the following year, 'in bad spirit, as if cricketers were enemies.' Perhaps another Australian report came closest to a summary text of this adventure. Of the game at Ballarat it briefly reported: 'The wicket played beautifully, the sun shone hotly; the XI scored tremendously; we fielded abominably; and all drank excessively.' Apart from the opening clause, it was a fair summation.

This was the time when Grace and Billy Midwinter crossed paths. Midwinter played twice for Victoria teams against Grace's team. In December 1873 he managed only 7, with Grace capturing his wicket. This was a three-day game watched by no less than 40,000 people. But some weeks later, in March 1874, he took 3 for 29, playing for a Victoria XVIII. 'Amidst the greatest enthusiasm' (the *Melbourne Standard*'s phrase) he clean-bowled both W.G. and his brother G.F.

Did W. G. Grace make a 'pact', as Benny Green called it (in an article in *The Observer*, 'Not Quite Cricket'), with W. E. Midwinter, so that, were he to come back to England, he would play for Gloucester? Certainly Benny Green believes that he did, and W.G. would have realized that Midwinter was Gloucester-born. There was some confusion about this, for there were claims that he was a true-born Aussie. H. S. Altham, usually the model of precision, labels him a Canadian, just to add to the mystery. Possibly Midwinter was later content to appear under one label or the other as it suited his purpose. Of course, in the previous summer season, the MCC had tightened up its birth-qualification rules, and it may have occurred to Grace to put in a word to the wise. On the other hand, these were Gloucestershire's finest seasons: they were, defiantly, an all-amateur, all-conquering combine. And, had W.G. fancied Midwinter's assistance, there is no reason why he should not have found the emigrant all-rounder willing to return then rather than in 1877.

As it was, Agnes and W. G. Grace retraced their seaward steps without him, fifty days of intermittent *mal de mer* and hands of whist stretching from Adelaide until, on 18 May, Southampton was reached. It was an unhappy sort of trip for a honeymoon: there was, among the feasting and jollification, a little too much rancour. There had even been suggestions that Grace cheated in regard of his fees, and it was a full twenty seasons before he returned to Australia. The English were, in part, unpopular, just as the Australians were, in part, despised. At the same time, there was genuine admiration and friendliness on both sides. It was the start of a long and traditional rivalry, and W. G. Grace was, for good and ill, its chief progenitor. He was but a twenty-five-year-old medical student, but he bestrode the cricketing globe like a colossus.

W. G. GRACE: HIS LIFE AND TIMES, *George Allen & Unwin, 1981*

— 3 —

PRESCRIPTIONS INDOORS AND OUT

The Doctor

A. A. THOMSON

THE medical registration examination he [W.G.] passed was that of Durham University. He then studied, as his father and brothers had done, at the Bristol Medical School and afterwards did his practical training at St. Bartholomew's and Westminster Hospital. For two years after his return, with his bride, from the extended honeymoon of his first Australian tour, he studied at Bart's under Howard Marsh and A. E. Cumberbatch. For a short time after that he stayed with his brother Henry at Kingswood and acted as his assistant. When the young couple returned to London they lived first in Earls Court and then in Acton and W.G. 'walked' the wards at Westminster Hospital under the famous Dr. Allchin. It was the work done at the Westminster which enabled him to qualify for his L.R.C.P. By the end of the year 1879 he had become a Licentiate of the Royal College of Physicians at Edinburgh – this was the diploma of the Tom Emmett story – as well as Member of the Royal College of Surgeons (England).

For the greater part of the next twenty years he followed his profession in Bristol both as parish doctor and as general practitioner to a large working-class practice. This practice was large enough for him to employ an assistant all the year round and a locum during the cricket season. Without labouring the point, it may be said that he did not neglect his patients for his cricket. Summer's lease hath all too short a date and the official cricket season is not a long one. If W.G. practised batting in his garden on a cold February morning or played an occasional Saturday afternoon game in October, no patient suffered. Even in the height of the season, he always liked to be home from his cricket for the week-end. Once he was back in Bristol he could not keep away from his patients, and he put in a great deal of work on Saturday and Sunday evenings. The county club made him an allowance towards the expense of paying a locum. The allowance, which was at first fixed at £20 and afterwards increased to £36 as fixtures became more frequent, is hardly evidence of a grasping nature in its recipient.

Whatever his bedside manner may have been, his crease-side manner was unexceptionable. Once E. M. (Joe) Hadow made a running catch at deep square-leg to dismiss W.G. and, unable to check his career, stumbled forward to fall with his head against the projecting metal edge of a stand. On his way back to the pavilion W.G. paused and administered first aid with a gentler firmness than he could reasonably have been expected to display towards a man who had just caught him off a hit that should have been a six.

Palmer, the old Kent wicketkeeper, was badly cut over the eye by a fast bumper which had just whistled past W.G.'s head. Efficiently if painfully, the batsman stitched up the wound. When play was resumed, W.G. stepped out of his ground to hit a slow ball for six, missed it and was stumped. He gave the wicketkeeper a reproachful parting frown.

'After all I've done for you,' he growled, 'that's what you do to me . . .'

The most famous example of W.G.'s cricket doctoring involved the undoubted saving of life. The patient was A. C. M. Croome, the old Gloucestershire cricketer and cricket writer, who in the county's Lancashire match in 1887 had gashed his throat on one of the spiked railings in front of the pavilion at Old Trafford in a vain effort to save a four. The laceration was deep and while messengers were scurrying round Stretford to find a surgical needle to stitch it, W.G. held the jagged edges of the wound together. It was a matter of life and death that the injured parts should be kept perfectly still and the Doctor's hand never shook for one instant. He literally held the victim's life in his hand for nearly half an hour and such a feat would only have been possible to a man of his iron nerve and fantastic stamina. It would have been remarkable at any time but W.G. had been in the field all day and done a good deal of bowling, as he always did. That he should have held on without the slightest twitching of finger and thumb was something near a miracle.

The nerve and endurance displayed on that day were of greater value to the individual patient than any amount of tact and suavity, and there were few men and women among W.G.'s large working-class practice in the Stapleton Road district of Bristol who did not enjoy the advantages of these qualities and many others. Nothing seemed to tire him on his rounds any more than at the wicket. In the middle of a big innings against Middlesex he was up all night wrestling with a confinement. In the morning he came back to the Clifton ground to take his score to 221, at which point his No. 11 left him with the total at 348. Anyone else in the world would have felt entitled to a rest but not W.G. Bowling at one end with Woof at the other, he helped to rattle Middlesex out in time to win the game by an innings. In the match he took ten wickets for a song. Perhaps he had a good sleep on the third night.

Occasionally the emergency treatment given on the field was drastic rather than delicate. There was a young Kent amateur, C. J. M. Fox, who had an extraordinary unfortunate experience of what we may term the rougher end of the Grace osteopathy. Fox, fielding at point, stooped sharply to stop a hard hit and pitched heavily forward, putting his shoulder out. E.M., backing up at the bowler's end, ran to him, at the same time waving his bat towards the pavilion. Out bustled W.G. and the next scene presented to the astonished spectators was that of E.M. sitting on the head of his prey while W.G., grabbing an arm, began to pull, with his foot as a fulcrum. There was an agonizing pause. Then a loud crack, as the shoulder went back into place, announced that the Graces had done their job. 'You're a very lucky young man!' cried W.G. It was a rough bit of Bob-Sawyer-like surgery, but it worked.

This slightly macabre incident had an unbelievable sequel. Two or three years later the thing happened again, like a second performance of a Grand Guignol play. The unfortunate Fox fell and put his shoulder out. E.M. rushed to the rescue. There was only one absentee, and that was W.G. himself, who did not happen to be playing. Two Kent colleagues were called on to sit on the patient's head, while E.M. performed the ferocious pump-handling. Desperate ailments need desperate remedies but the Grace remedies were seldom as desperate as that. Rough-and-ready as such incidents may occasionally have been, W.G. did not gain the respect and affection of a large part of the working population of Bristol by mere rough-and-ready methods. His physical strength, his unshakeable confidence, his steadiness, as experienced by Croome, and, above all, his buoyant, boyish humour: all these qualities are desirable in any man; in a doctor their worth is untold. Without exaggeration it is possible to think of him as almost the ideal doctor for this kind of general work: big, bluff, cheerful, imperturbable, friendly but not too sympathetic; widely experienced in everyday ailments. He was frankly no specialist, but an admirable general practitioner.

Since W.G.'s day medical science has made enormous strides in drugs and radiological treatment, but not in the personal responsibility of the individual doctor, who tends to pass his patients into hospital with all the nervous haste of a scrum-half menaced by wing-forwards. The attitude of modern medicine towards the general practitioner is one of amused condescension. There is a specialist for most ailments, and if we cannot fit our ailments to the available specialists, we are made to feel that we are somehow culpable . . .

His [W.G.'s] patients admired him without hysteria. He had neither the passion for healing nor the saintliness of character which gave a man the title of Beloved Physician. But he was magnificently equipped with the middle virtues: kindness, patience, good humour and that general practitioner's standby, common sense. He was to his patients, as to his cricketing opponents, something outside nature, a genuine nonesuch. Tom Emmett said W.G. ought to have a 'littler bat'. There is no record of any of his patients demanding that he should have a smaller stethoscope, yet, as has been frequently recorded, he seemed to many of them a kind of outsize Santa Claus. The people who afterwards recounted tales of their doctor were mostly simple, unsophisticated folk and their stories often ended with a typical line: 'He was a good gentleman, with no pride whatever.'

The stories of his doctoring are almost as many as of his cricket, but they are not so varied: running through them all is a thread of gruff kindness and unsentimental competence. Dressed in a roughish tweed suit with his blackthorn stick under his arm, he would walk briskly along the streets of his 'parish', sometimes reading his newspaper and sometimes pausing gravely to converse with stray children and dogs. If a family was short of fuel or food, he would rather grumpily produce a bag of coals or a basin of soup, as though out of a conjurer's hat. He would also take delight in bullying some friend of his into giving an unemployed man a job. If he went into a house where an ample dinner was on the table he would sniff the air appreciatively and murmur: 'By jove, that smells good,' and sit down to eat with the family. In winter weather, when snowballs were flying, his top hat was an inevitable target, but, as you might imagine, he deemed attack the best form of defence and gave as good as he got. His pick-up was swift, his return deadly, and he always seemed to have plenty of ammunition. Roaring with laughter, he volleyed and thundered.

His practice lay in a district of Bristol subject to periodic flooding and when he saw the waters beginning to rise, he shrugged his shoulders, put on his fishing waders and set off on his rounds. When he found patients in bed on the menaced ground floor he picked them up without ceremony and carried them upstairs to the first floor. In the wild winter of 1888 the whole of the Frome Valley was a swirling torrent. W.G. was determined to visit a patient on the far side of the Monk Street bridge, which had become perilously impassable. He hailed a water police boat which, with a crew of a sergeant and four constables, was patrolling the flooded area, and managed to extract from them a promise to take him across. The very thought of crossing was frightening, because there was every risk of the boat's being dashed over or against the coping of the bridge, but, 'Now, boys, for it,' cried W.G., and over they went. When you think of the extra weight of bone, muscle and determination they had taken aboard, you will agree that all five policemen merited a medal.

He was occasionally eccentric in his prescriptions. Throughout the course of an influenza epidemic he was called out at all hours of the twenty-four and there came a time when he was feeling extremely short of sleep. An anxious husband threw stones at his window in the middle of the night, and, when the window was opened, described his wife's symptoms at great length. 'Go away!' W.G. called out at last; 'I'll see her in the morning. She'll be all right till then if you'll warm her half a pint of old beer!' Then the great bearded silhouette retreated from its frame and the window was banged down.

To a mildly drunken sweep who had beerily demanded a tonic, W.G. replied: 'What you want, my lad, is exercise, not medicine.' He then called to the maid: 'Mary, fetch me those boxing gloves.' At that the patient rushed out of the surgery in terror, crying out as he ran down the street: 'The great big b—— wants to fight me!'

THE GREAT CRICKETER, *Hale, 1957*

WITH reference to a sentence which has become classical, the one uttered by J. C. Shaw – but erroneously attributed on occasions to Alfred Shaw – W.G. Grace himself must be quoted:

'My experience of J. C. Shaw was that at first he tried all he knew to get me out, but after I got set he was not quite so keen and gave me repeatedly a ball to hit for no other purpose than to get me to the other end so that he "might have a try at some one else", as he said. And over after over he bowled a wild ball in the hope of getting me caught; giving as his reason for doing it: "It ain't a bit of use my bowling good 'uns to him now; it is a case of I can bowl where I likes and he can hit where he likes." '

— 4 —

THE BIG'UN

Summer

A. A. THOMSON

THE momentous month of August 1876 is now upon the horizon. W.G. began on the old Argyle Street ground at Hull in a game for the United South *v.* the United North with one of those one-man performances which must have made the scorers wonder why he ever bothered to have any partners at all. While W.G. played superbly against hostile bowling, Pooley was making 14 and the next highest score was 4. Thus W.G. made 126 and ten others made 28 between them. In this innings he made several hits into the grounds of a nearby lunatic asylum and lifted one colossal drive into a passing railway truck, and thereby into history for the confusion of modern cricket brains trusts.

And here begins the story of the 11th to the 18th August, eight days which shook the cricket world. On 10th August he went down in blazing sunshine to his well-loved Canterbury to play in a twelve-a-side game for the M.C.C. against Kent. He spent the first day modestly, painstakingly leather-hunting while Kent piled up a huge score on the foundations of a finely hit century and a half by Lord Harris. Next day, doubtless worn out by their exertions, M.C.C. collapsed and had to follow on after tea with the hopeless task of getting well over 300 runs to save the innings defeat. W.G., as always, was rather anxious to get home to Downend that Saturday night and so hit out in his free style, not being much oppressed by any particular urge to stay in. But so true was the wicket, so hard (though never reckless) was his hitting that in forty-five minutes he had scored his hundred and at close of play was 133 not out.

Next day, as he recalls, he was 'busy'. Runs flowed from his bat in a turbulent torrent. Partners came and went until, very near the call of time, he was caught for 344 out of a total of 546. William Yardley, who spent the whole time in the field against him, confessed that, in every sense, it was the hottest time he was ever likely to experience — in this world, at any rate.

W.G. did not get his Saturday rest and spent most of his Sunday in the train on the stifling cross-country journey to Bristol, but by Monday morning he was ready to turn out at Clifton for Gloucestershire, to win the toss, roll up his sleeves and under a hot sun put his old friends from Nottingham to the sword with a score of 177. He called this innings the filling in the eight-day sandwich, not because it was meatier, but because, as in railway refreshment rooms, it was smaller than the other two slices.

He had not far to go for his third game, which was played at Cheltenham. There is a story that the Notts men, travelling back to Trent Bridge after their hammering, met the Yorkshiremen coming down from the north on Cheltenham railway station and gave them a graphic account of what W.G. had been doing.

'Maybe you're right,' chuckled Tom Emmett, 'but afore we'd let him knock us about like that against Yorkshire, we'd shooit him. Even t'Big 'Un couldn't do it three times.'

But in those eight days the Big 'Un could do anything. He was insatiable and inexorable. He could win the toss, bat all the first day, and after the unexpected rain had stopped on the second day, go on to hammer the Yorkshire bowlers not merely into exhaustion but into insubordination. As he had approached the wicket at the beginning of his innings, he had said genially to Tom Emmett: 'You'll have to get me out today. I shan't get myself out!' Nor did he. The bowlers suffered total subjugation. They toiled, they sweated and then they mutinied. When their captain, Ephraim Lockwood, an amiable but hardly commanding personality, asked Allan Hill to come back and bowl, he begged to be let off.

'Make him bowl,' cried Tom Emmett. 'Tha'rt captain.'

'Bowl him thi-sen, Tom,' retorted Allan. 'Tha'rt frightened.'

Whereupon Tom picked up the ball and delivered in succession three of the widest wides that even he had ever sent down. In Yorkshire they like to pretend that Tom then bowled his opponent with a 'sostenutor'. But the grim fact remains that at the end of the innings W.G.'s score stood at not out 318, the highest individual total in county cricket until A. C. MacLaren broke the record twenty years later. In eight days W.G. had made 839 with an average, as he liked to boast, of 419½.

In July a game, not technically termed first class, took place at Grimsby between United South and a local Twenty-Two. Before the match the Grimsby captain complained that the eleven brought by W.G. was not strong enough. This was a little hard, seeing that, besides W.G. himself, Fred Grace and their cousin W. R. Gilbert, the side contained Jupp, Humphrey, and the redoubtable Pooley. It was also a factual error.

At the end of the first day the visitors had scored 217 for two (W.G. 136 not out, Fred 39 not out). There were twenty-two fielders and W.G. played unmercifully on the weakest of them. He wore brown pads – were these Alfred Mynn's? – and at the end of the second day he had made 314.

A tribute to the presence of twenty-two fieldsmen and to W.G.'s almost superhuman endurance lay in the fact that his innings, when everybody else was out, contained 158 singles. Only the centre of the ground was closely cut and, time and again, W.G.'s hits were slowed down in the long grass. His innings also contained four sixes and twenty-one fours, but the ceaseless stream of singles was the true sign of stamina. There was one break in the flow, however. Towards the end of the second day a telegram arrived, announcing that Mrs. W.G. had been safely delivered of her second son. Right through W.G.'s life there were certain occasions thought worthy of champagne. This was one of them and he invited both sides to toast the new child of Grace. In Grimsby they still swear that W.G.'s final score was not what appears in the records. When the last wicket fell at 681, W.G. came towards the pavilion and called up to the scoring-box — there was, of course, no running indication of individual scores:

'What did I get?'

'Three-ninety-nine,' the scorer called back.

'Oh, make it four hundred,' laughed W.G.

And the scorer, who believed that something should be done to celebrate an innings of 399 and the birth of a happy baby, replied: 'All right, then, you certainly deserve it!'

And that is how W.G.'s score appears in all the records as 400 not out. Or so they will tell you in Grimsby.

Again the writers for the comic papers showed their awe in protective facetiousness. The periodical *Funny Folks* gave a burlesque account of a cricket match:

'W.G.'s first stroke was a clean square hit to leg for 34. At three o'clock two more went down with sunstroke while umbrellas were supplied to those remaining. Score 1,142. At half-past three W.G. ate an Abernethy biscuit and anchovy, but declined drinks. Thermometer 98. Bowlers changed every five minutes. Fielders now reduced to eight men – the score at 1,366 . . . W.G. carried out his bat for 2,001 by as fine an exhibition of all-round cricket as we would wish to see. He had been at the wickets exactly twelve hours, and declared himself in readiness to go in the next day, but the Wapshots declined. I forgot to say that eleven bats were broken during the match.'

THE GREAT CRICKETER, *Hale, 1957*

'W.G.'

THERE's a name which will live for ever and aye
    In the true-born cricketer's mind –
A name which is loudly re-echoed to-day,
    And borne on the wings of the wind;
Britannia may gladly be proud of her sons,
    Since who is more famous than he,
The stalwart compiler of thousands of runs,
    'Leviathan' W.G.?

His home is the turf where the wicket is pitched,
    And there in defence he stands,
The heart of the willow is fairly bewitched
    As soon as it touches his hands.
All useless the efforts of Emmett and Hill –
    No bowler of any degree
Can check the effect of the magical will
    Of 'marvellous' W.G.

The eagle he rivals in keennes of eye,
    So sure his defence and attack;
Each bailer and shooter he seems to defy
    And sends the curly ones back.
While all the assemblage in wonderment fix
    Their eyes on his well-placed three,
Oh! follow the flight of the ponderous six
    Oh 'wonderful' W.G. . . .

Played at the Grimsby Cricket Ground, July 10th, 11th and 12th, 1876, in which the champion 'bat' scored the extraordinary number of 400 runs, which include 4 sixes.

All England Cricket and Football Journal, *1877.*

FROM THE HORSE'S MOUTH

Interview with Mr W. G. Grace,
M.R.C.S., L.R.C.P.

F.W.W.

THROUGHOUT the extent of the British Empire, be it north, south, east, or west, more this season, perhaps, than in any other, has the name of Mr. William Gilbert Grace become a household word. Be it peer or peasant, all unite in doing homage to the hero of a hundred 'centuries' – the man who has done more to further the progress of the grand old English game than any other man of this or any other time; and, although he reached the age of forty-seven in July last (a period when a cricketer is generally supposed to become superfluous upon the field), Mr. Grace is yet the man who is considered the most dangerous of any side, not alone by our English teams, but by visitors from the Antipodes. No matter what the ground may be, hard or soft, when the champion walks to his place at the wickets, who is to say when he will be again sent back to the pavilion?

And this is the position which he has occupied since so long ago as 1866, when at the age of eighteen, he set the cricket world a-wondering by his innings of 224 not out, for England *versus* Surrey. From then until now he has stood head and shoulders above all other contemporary batsmen; he has seen younger blood infused into the county teams, and go again, yet he is now capable of as much endurance upon the grassy sward as any . . .

I was fortunate enough to meet him as he stepped off the field at Lord's a few weeks back with the plaudits of the spectators, in recognition of his innings of 125 for the M.C.C. against Kent, yet ringing in the air. But with kindliness and good-fellowship beaming from every line of his bronzed and bearded face, the champion grasped my hand with a grip which made me wince again, and acceded to my request for a few minutes' chat on past and present cricket. With the kindly 'burr' of the west country tongue lingering on every sentence, he told me how he was born at Downend, near Bristol, on July 18th, 1848, and, plunging at once into the thread of his story, went on to speak of the first match he recollected watching, at that time a wee lad of six, seated upon his father's knee.

'That was when I saw the All England Eleven play against Twenty-two of West Gloucestershire, at Bristol,' he remarked, '. . . That, as I was telling you, was the first match I can remember seeing, but as years went on I believe that I was present at every match I possibly could get at. And all the time my brothers and myself were being coached by my uncle, Mr. Pocock, into the rudiments of the game.

'He was a great enthusiast in the game, you know, and taught us the correct style, and when I was old enough I used to play for the West Gloucestershire Club, of which my father was the manager. Unfortunately, however, we had no ground at Downend, and had to play upon the common, about a mile away; but we lads when at home used to pitch our wickets in the orchard. That was where I first got a knowledge of the game.

'The first match I played in? Well, that was when I was nine years old, and I scored 3 not out. I played three more innings that year, I remember, and scored only another single. That wasn't exactly great, was it? Nor were my records exactly as I wished for the next few years. . . .

'But all this time, you must remember, I was still practising under Uncle Pocock's eye, while beyond cricket we boys also went in for the kite carriages, of which he was the inventor. Of course, this is really outside the game, but I may mention that we used to beat the carriages drawn by horses frequently, while on one occasion he raced and defeated the Duke of York's carriage on the London Road. That was his recreation, you know; but to get back to cricket again. I left school in 1863, and after a very severe illness I was placed under the charge of a tutor by my father. That season I played nineteen innings, and hit up 350 runs, being not out on six occasions, and securing an average of 26.

'By this time, as you may imagine, I was getting pretty well known as a cricketer in the neighbourhood of Bristol, and had scored 18 and 1 in the match Gentlemen of Gloucester v. Gentlemen of Devon. But it was not until '64 that I accomplished my first great performance. I was only fifteen at that time, mind you, but a big boy for my age, and playing for the Gentlemen of South Wales against the Gentlemen of Sussex made 170 and 56 not out, and took two wickets in the first innings. This success led to my being requested to play in the following year for the Gentlemen *v.* the Players both at Lord's and the Oval. I did fairly well, but the first century I ever hit up in first-class cricket was made in 1866. England was playing Surrey, at the Oval, and, going in fifth for the former, I did not come out again until I had made 224, and then was not out.

'Since then I have been playing continually in first-class cricket whenever I have been available and eligible, although at times my duties precluded all idea of my donning the flannels. In the field I used to prefer being placed at long leg, but I much prefer point now. Eighteen stone, for that is what I have weighed for a good many years past, is quite enough for me to carry when batting, and I can tell you I don't care for sprinting to the boundary in the attempt to save a four as much as I did in my younger days.

'What was my best year with the bat? Well (with a laugh) I have had so many that I almost forget, but I think you may be safe in saying that I was most successful in 1870. In that season I had 35 innings, scoring 2,739 runs, and having an average of 78 at the close. With these figures you may perhaps think I had a little luck with the bowlers. But I don't think I had. I know I had to face J. C. Shaw, Alfred Shaw, Southerton, Martin McIntyre, and Wooton, and they were all good men.

'Then my best season with the ball, I think, was in 1867. I took 39 wickets at a cost of 6·21 each; in 1874 I secured 129 for 12; 1875, 192 for 12; and again in 1877 the same average, 179 for 12. My highest innings, I may add was that scored in 1876 against Twenty-two of Grimsby and District for a United South of England Eleven. When we went on the ground they grumbled because we had brought a weak team, but there wasn't much said after I made 400, not out, out of 681, and was at the wickets until nearly four o'clock on the third day. But this performance was never an actual record, you know. A few weeks after I had made the runs I have just mentioned, I made 344 for Gentlemen of M.C.C. against Kent, followed with 179 *v.* Notts, and 318 not out *v.* Yorkshire.

'Beyond these performances, I have three times scored over a hundred in each innings, and, with Mr. B. B. Cooper, made a record of 283 for the first wicket for Gentlemen of the South against Players of the South. This stood as a record until it was beaten by Messrs. H. T. Hewett and L. C. Palairet at Taunton, playing for Somersetshire *v.* Yorkshire. As to what I should call the best of my innings – well, you must judge that for yourself.

'And now to present-day cricket. Well, I think myself that the players who were known when I first came out would fairly hold their own now, while in many cases I fancy they might be better. Of course, we hadn't the pitches then that we have now, and every hit was run out. The consequence of this was that perhaps a batsman would get excited in trying to get a six, with a short run as the last, and the field had a better chance of running him out than they have at the present day.

'Why, there were no boundaries at the time I am speaking of, and at Lord's and the Oval, if the ball didn't go inside the pavilion we had to run it out. This is what makes me think that it is easier to get a hundred now than it was then. The only remedy that I know for this would be to put a wooden fence right round the playing ground, say some 2 ft. high. If a ball should be sent over, it should be a boundary, and count the regulation four; if not, it should be run out.

'Of course, the reason these boundaries were established had nothing to do with saving the batsmen. It was the crowd who had to be considered, for I have seen a fieldsman knock down four or five spectators when going after a ball. We used to go right in, and let everybody take care of himself. As regards the question whether batting and bowling are improving, of course, there are a great many more players now than there were twenty and twenty-five years ago, but I don't think there is much difference.

'The players, I am bound to admit, are stronger in bowling than the amateurs, but I think I can explain that. An amateur does not appear to care for bowling so much as for batting. And then, again, a professional does not go on for so many years. You hear of them, as a general rule, for a few seasons, and then they give up the game and go into business. But with amateurs the case is very different. They play solely for the love of the thing itself, and keep on year after year, and season after season.

'Not much difference in University cricket? No, I can't say that there is, although taken as a whole it is better now than it used to be. And the same may be said of public school cricket, although with the latter I should like to point out one thing. That is this: There is a tendency to keep a boy down to a certain style in his play. He must play the "correct game," it is said; but suppose a lad has an ugly style, and yet is a hitter who can get runs, why should he not be coached up in that? Instead of that, however, he is taught how to hold his bat by the regulation rule and the result is that instead of being a fearless slogger he is to a great measure spoilt. These remarks, I may as well say, apply equally to the bowling as to the batting.

'My opinion is that, provided a lad is able to keep his wicket up and to get runs, although his style may not be a pretty one for a spectator to watch, he should be allowed to play his own game, under certain not too strict conditions, of course. When at the Universities the style of a young player has been practically formed, but it would be as well if the men were to practise bowling more than they do just now. But I suppose the reason why the ball is not so favoured as the bat is by reason of the wicket being much easier now than was the case when I first remember them. Now, almost every college at both Oxford and Cambridge has grounds of its own, and there is ample opportunity for them to turn out good teams. I should not say that upon the average there is much difference between either 'Varsity eleven, but you must remember that Fenners is much easier for the batsmen, and correspondingly more difficult for the bowlers, than the parks at Oxford. I should say that is why the Cantabs are not so very strong as a rule in the latter department for it takes all the heart out of a man to send down over after over, day after day, without getting a wicket. As regards the best bowlers I have met at Cambridge, I might mention R. M. Powys, A. G. Steel, S. M. J. Woods, F. S. Jackson.

'But it is not exactly fair to judge the capability of a team from their display upon a London ground. For one thing, the batsmen are far from being at home under the altered conditions. The men are nervous, too, especially if it should be their first appearance in London.

'And as regards the admission of additional counties into the championship series: this I do not think is exactly an improvement. With so many teams engaged it will be found impossible to play home and home matches with each county. The consequences of this may be that, perhaps, some strong counties will only meet some of the weaker ones; and then again, matters may get so complicated when the points come to be calculated that there will be a difficulty in really finding out who are the champions.

'Then there is another thing I am afraid of. That is, that cricket will be made too much of a business, like football – with the consequences that none but professionals will be seen playing. That, I hope, will not come in our times; but there is that probability to be faced. Should such a condition of affairs occur – well, betting and all other kindred evils will follow in its wake, and instead of the game being followed up for love, it will simply be a matter of £ s. d.

'And then there is another thing that militates against the well-being of a team. That is the behaviour of the crowd. If a batsman is unfortunate, there is always a section of the public who starts jeering as soon as he may come in. That takes all the confidence out of a man, and if he should be an amateur, he would not stand it for long. Then, again, if a fieldsman fails to take a difficult chance, or is slow in a return, the crowd set about him again. But I can tell you a man feels quite bad enough when he knows he has missed a chance of sending an opponent back, without having the spectators howling at him. You can't expect anyone to stand too much of this kind of treatment, and if things should reach a climax, the gentlemen always have a remedy in their own hands. All they will have to do will be to give up the county games, form clubs, and decide fixtures amongst themselves.

'How do I think the alteration in the rule of follow-on will affect the game, you ask. That all depends; and as it has been afforded such a short trial, I prefer not to say too much upon the subject; but I think it may make the game a little fairer for the fielding side. Say their opponents complete their first innings, and then have to follow on. Well, the chances are all in favour of a big score being knocked up. The bowlers and fieldsmen are fatigued, while the batsmen have had an opportunity of resting themselves. With the margin enlarged to 120 runs, however, it should tend to make the game of a more equal character, for it is not often that an eleven would fall so far in the rear as that figure.

'Then you mention the "retired hurt" question, that has provoked such a discussion since the pronouncement of the secretary of the M.C.C. Of course, if a batsman is hurt he retires, and then may come out again and finish his innings if an arrangement is made with the opposing captain. As for saying that a player might retire under what practically would mean false pretences for the sake of his average, that cannot be taken into serious consideration for a moment. A man would never do that – that is my experience of the game; and if he should do so by any chance, well, he wouldn't be played again, you may depend upon that.

'Now, that is hardly a fair question to ask.'

This in reply to a question of mine respecting which ground in England was the best, in Mr. Grace's opinion.

'All county grounds are good; some are naturally slower than others, but no fault can be found with the manner in which they are kept. But if you want to know which is the easiest ground from a batsman's point of view, I should certainly pitch upon that at Brighton. There is a very small boundary there, it is fast, and a team ought to be able to score a hundred a day there in advance of the figures they might obtain upon some other grounds.

'But I think that on the whole Australian wickets are better, as a rule, than ours. They have all the climatic advantages necessary to make a pitch something like what we were getting in May and June of this year. At Melbourne, Adelaide, and Sydney the grounds are as good as ours, as level as a billiard table, and much easier to score upon owing to their being so fast. But it doesn't follow from this that a player who has made a big reputation home here would do well at the Antipodes. For one thing, the climate is liable to upset a visitor, and then the glare of the sun exercises a dazzling effect upon one, which you are a considerable time in getting used to.

'In America they also have fairly good grounds; that was how I found it when I was across there, and I dare say they have improved matters considerably since then. But the cricket is only about as good as that of the weakest of our counties, although the clubs are so enthusiastic over the game, that negotiations have been opened for the visit of a couple of our teams some time during the present season. But there is really no comparison between English and Colonial cricket. Why, here, at home, we ought to beat Australia every time, although when you take a team out there, there is a certainty that it would not be a really representative one. The matters I have already mentioned would militate against its success, while the hospitality is too much for good play.

'There is, however, one feature of the Australian cricket which I may perhaps mention. They have had a really wonderful succession of first-class bowlers in a short time. The batting, when the number of players is considered in proportion, is not nearly so good; but as they have so very few professionals, the amateurs are forced to handle the leather themselves. In the big matches and club fixtures, the latter more especially, I have found that the trundling is better there than in England.

'But I have met some capital bowlers in the past. I should class them in two sections, the slows including A. Shaw, Peate, Southerton, Mr. A. G. Steel, Watson, Mr. Buchanan; and the fasts – Freeman, Tarrant, Jackson, Hill, Willsher, Morley, J. C. Shaw, Mr. Tonge, and Mr. Appleby.

'I think myself that the bowling was quite as difficult when I came out in first-class cricket as at the present time; but amongst the most successful of the present time with the leather, I should put Peel, Briggs, and Mr. C. L. Townsend as the slows, and Mr. S. Woods, Mr. Kortright, Mold, Richardson, and Lockwood as the fasts.

'The consideration of the various degrees of excellence amongst the bowlers takes you, as a matter of course, to the consideration of throwing. I must admit that some of the very fast bowlers (I need mention no names) are looked upon with suspicion; but I really do not think they are any worse now than they were in years gone by. There was always a certain percentage of suspicion, and so, I suppose, it will have to go on. There is one thing certain, and that is, you will never get an umpire to no-ball a suspicious bowler who is allowed to take part in present cricket.

'The only remedy I can suggest would be for a dozen umpires and a similar number of captains of the best county teams to meet together. The names of all the bowlers who were suspected of throwing should be placed upon a slip of paper. Then they should be marked, as by ballot, whether they were considered to throw or not, the decision of a two-thirds majority to be final, and if a man were convicted of throwing he should not be allowed to bowl again. That is the only way in which the evil could be coped with, in my opinion, and when a man knew that he might be debarred from further play – well, it would make him much more careful.

'Then another thing that is often asked me is, whether I think football improves a man for cricket. No, I do not. A man cannot do well at cricket unless he has followed the game up all his life, while I could mention Rugby forwards who really run away from fast bowlers. A cricketer, however, should take plenty of exercise to keep himself fit during the winter. But people have much over-rated the methods I pursue. You read of all kinds of means, but you may take it from me that they are, in the majority of instances, untrue.

'Last winter I was certainly out once or twice a week with the Clifton Foot Beagles, but I commenced practising much later this year than usual. But it doesn't follow that even if a man is in training he will do equally well at all times. A spell of bad luck may unsettle him, or a biting east wind may take all the suppleness out of his joints. A man who plays cricket, and cricket alone, though, is not likely to make a shining light. Exercise is what you require. If you can't run you can ride, and if you can't ride you can walk.

'This reminds me that I was never defeated over hurdles at 200 yds., while my favourite distance on the flat was a quarter of a mile. But I have been credited with covering 100 yds. in $10\frac{4}{5}$ sec., and clearing 5 ft. in the high jump, while I remember one instance in which there was an amusing dispute with by brother, E.M. You must know that he could beat me in a 100 yds. sprint, but we both entered for the event and got on the mark. I kept one eye upon the starter and, poaching a couple of yards at the pistol shot, won by a foot. E.M. wouldn't speak to me after this for a time, but the coolness soon wore off with the dear old fellow. But I never possessed any style in my running. When I came out at sixteen I was unmercifully chaffed at the way I threw my legs and arms about, but I persevered, and at last, two years later, won the 300 yds. strangers' race at Clifton College sports.'

Upon turning up the records, it may be mentioned *en passant* that in 1869 he had gained the reputation of being one of the fastest quarter-mile runners in England, and in 1870, when giving racing up, had gained over seventy cups and medals. In 1866 Mr. Grace secured eighteen 1sts and two 2nds; 1867, one 1st; 1868, six 1sts; 1869, seventeen 1sts, nine 2nds, and one 3rd; and in 1870, five 1sts, one 2nd, and one 3rd. His best times were: 100 yds., upon grass, $10\frac{4}{5}$ sec.; 150 yds. (with 5 yds. start), $15\frac{1}{2}$ sec.; 200 yds. hurdles, 28 sec.; 440 yds. flat race, $52\frac{1}{5}$

sec.; long jump, 17½ ft.; high jump, 5 ft.; hop, step, and jump, 41 ft.; pole jump, 9 ft.; and throwing the cricket ball, 122 yds. These figures will give an idea of what he was capable of at his best.

'How should I advise a young beginner to start learning the game? That is a somewhat difficult question, for every player possesses a style more or less distinctive. But the great thing for a youngster to secure is a good coach, who will teach him the correct way in which to hold his bat and take up his position at the wickets. Perhaps a lad may say that the hard and fast rules may make him feel cramped and stiff at the wicket, but you may depend upon it that he will soon adapt himself to the various conditions. Then, in taking his place against the bowler, the batsman should be particular in seeing that he plays with a perfectly straight bat, while his toes should be just outside an imaginary line drawn from the leg and off stump of each wicket respectively. This will enable him to get well over his work, while he will stand less chance of being bowled off his pads.

'As for the position in which to stand, there is no hard and fast rule, but what I generally favour is the placing of the left leg about 12 in. in front and at right angles to my other. The right foot should come inside the crease, and as a general rule should not be moved. Shift your left foot as much as you like when batting, but upon the right depends the stability of your defence. If you are continually shifting it, you will get out very soon.

'And now for the bat. No doubt you have observed the peculiarity of many players in respect of the length of the handle. Some have long, others again have them shorter. I myself prefer a handle of the ordinary length, and hold it about half-way up. Then you must keep your eye upon the bowler until the instant when the ball leaves his hand, for you can generally tell by this in which way he intends to break. Then you should make the bat hit the ball, not let the ball hit the bat.

'If you make up your mind to hit, hit hard, half measures are of no use; and when you block, put just a little power into your strokes. You should not be content to stop the ball by simply interposing the bat, but play it in such a manner that runs may be secured. Hit hard, then: that is my advice to a young player; but get well over the ball and never spoon it up. A hit travels much farther when it is kept down than when sent high in the air; while it is but seldom found that a slogger, who skies all his hits, scores many runs.

'With regard to the various styles of play, it is difficult to advise. You see, each player generally has a different method, and a long-reached man will be able to get forward and smother a ball that shorter-reached batsmen can only play by getting further back. There is consequently much that must be left to individual judgment, but I should most strongly caution a player against betraying a tendency to play across the wicket, or to pull balls. A leg ball that is a leg ball should be hit to leg, but young players are only too apt to attempt to pull almost every ball sent down. The result of this is that they fail to do much in the game owing to their faulty style.

'In cutting, you should never fail to keep the ball down, patting it down, if I may use the expression, although nothing but practice will bring the familiarity necessary for the playing of the game. You should practise frequently and play as carefully at the nets as in an actual match; while many useful hints may be learnt by watching the best players. A beginner, mind you, should not be a copyist, but there is more to be learnt in half an hour's actual practice than can be taught in a week of theory.

'And now we come to bowling. In this department too much attention cannot be given, although the young beginner should not attempt to bowl fast at first. If he does, possibly he will sacrifice pitch and straightness. Commencing, say, at 18 yards instead of 22, he should gradually work his way back to the longer distance, and by placing a mark, easily seen, upon the pitch at a certain distance from the wicket, he will soon be able to vary his length at will, and bowl somewhere near the spot aimed at. Trying to twist the ball should only come after a man has learnt to bowl straight. To accomplish this the ball should be held firmly in the hand, with the fingers grasping it well over the centre and resting over the seams. Then in leaving go, the fingers should relax their grasp, imparting the twist so destructive to the unwary batsman.

'But there is more to be gained by altering your pace and length than by bowling dead upon the wicket time after time. Many batsmen will simply play maiden after maiden if the bowling is straight, but if you give them a few balls on either side of the wicket, it is probable that they will give a chance and be out. Of course, this does not apply to a poor batsman. He cannot play straight bowling for any length of time, and is bound to let the ball beat him eventually.

'Which is the best bowling, fast or slow? Well, that depends upon the ground. Although a fast bowler upon a good wicket is the easiest to score from, my eye is not so sure as it was at one time, and I think I prefer a medium-paced ball myself. Considering the two styles of bowling, however, slow is generally the best upon a soft wicket, and fast upon a hard, difficult pitch.

'Now, in conclusion, we come to the fielding. It is as much by activity in this department that a match is won as with the bat, for, if catches are missed, returns muffed, and runs allowed to be stolen – well, the bowlers will be sadly handicapped. Each man in the field should be intent upon the game, and nothing else. Talking during the over should not be allowed. A fieldsman should invariably run in to a ball, and not wait for it to come to him, while he can never tell what catches he may bring off unless he makes the attempt.

'One curious thing that is sometimes seen is that a poor field may take a catch coming off the bat at a tremendous pace, while he may miss an easy one. When making a catch off a swift ball, the hands should "give" a few inches involuntarily, but with a slow the ball is apt to jump out of your grip before the fingers can close round it.

'Then there is another point worth attention. Suppose you miss a ball. The best do this at times, but never lose a moment in vain regrets, but sprint off and save the runs. Then in returning the ball, unless you have an excellent reason, never throw to the bowler's end. When returning from the long field send the ball low and straight. The greater the curve, the longer it takes to reach the wicket, and the less chance is there of running the batsman out. By the due observance of these rules, there is no reason, if a young player is possessed of a good eye and head, why he should not prove a successful exponent of our noble game.

'There is one thing, however, in addition to these I have already enumerated, that has been discussed considerably; that is, upon either a wet or drying wicket, if you are successful in the toss, should you put your opponents in or have first knock yourself? The latter, most decidedly, I should say; for in this climate of ours you can never be certain of the weather for two days in succession. In fact, I may safely say that only about one in thirty or forty times does the experiment of putting your opponents in first prove successful.'

THE STRAND MAGAZINE, *1895*

HE SAID, I WROTE

Collaborating with W. G. Grace

ARTHUR PORRITT

MY happiest days in journalism, I think, were the cricket seasons of 1890 and 1891, when I was writing descriptive reports of cricket in London for the *Manchester Examiner*, and following the Lancashire team on its southern tours. A day in the Press box at a first class county match is still a long drawn out ecstasy to me. For a time I was thrown among cricketers, amateur and professional, and found them sterling, healthy-minded, large-hearted men with scarcely an exception. For George Lohmann I had a great affection. But the cricketer with whom I was brought into closest contact was the incomparable W. G. Grace.

I spent all the leisure of twelve months, some years later, working in collaboration with Dr. Grace on his well-known book, *W. G.: Cricketing Reminiscences*. It is not a breach of faith now to say that I wrote the book. Grace was choke full of cricketing history, experience and reminiscences, but he was a singularly inarticulate man, and had he been left to write his own cricketing biography it would never have seen the light. My friend Mr. James Bowden (through Mr. Coulson Kerna-han) sought my co-operation with Grace, who had entered into an agreement with him to produce a volume of reminiscences for publica-tion in his jubilee year. It had seemed as if the contract would expire without a line of the book having been writen. Grace accepted me as his collaborator with the utmost heartiness, and, although the task of getting the material from him was almost heartbreaking, I enjoyed the work immensely. My plan was to spend three half-days a week with W.G. in his own study – he was living at Sydenham then – and by every conceivable artifice that an experienced interviewer could bring into operation, lure him into a flow of reminiscence. Many days I drew a blank and came away with scarcely sufficient material for a paragraph. On other days I managed to enveigle him into a reminiscent vein, and he would send me off with data enough for one or two chapters.

W. G. Grace's mind functioned oddly. He never stuck to any train of recollection, but would jump from an event in the 'sixties to something that happened in, say, the last Test Match. Often I left his house in absolute despair. Once, at least, I asked leave to abandon the enterprise; but I was urged to persist. I remember very distinctly one age-long afternoon when I was trying to get out of W.G. something of the psychology of a batsman making a big score in a great match. All that he wanted to say in recording some dazzling batting feat of his own was, 'Then I went in and made 284.' 'Yes,' I would reply, 'but that is not good enough. People want to know what W. G. Grace felt like when he was doing it; what thoughts he had and what the whole mental experience of a big innings means to a batsman.' 'I did not feel anything; I had too much to do to watch the bowling and see how the fieldsmen were moved about to think anything.' The very best that I could get out of him was that 'some days a batsman's eye is *in* and other days it is not. When his eye is *in*, the cricket ball seems the size of a football and he can't miss it. When his eye isn't *in* then he isn't in long, because he's soon bowled out.'

I failed utterly, I confess, to draw from W.G. anything adequate in the way of a chapter on the art of cricket captaincy. He had the generalship of the game by instinct, and, in his autocratic fashion, was a sound captain with every artifice at his finger-tips. But he had no consciousness of what he did know in that department of cricket strategy – which, it must be remembered, was an empirical matter and not the exact science to which Australian captaincy has reduced it. So his advice to captains in his reminiscences is poor stuff. I could get nothing out of him that was in the slightest degree illuminating or helpful.

Conscious of his own inarticulateness, Grace was fearfully apprehensive lest I should put into his reminiscences any words that were not in his accustomed vocabulary. One day in running through a chapter I had written and which we were revising together, he pulled up at the word 'inimical'. 'No,' he said firmly, 'that word can't go in. Why, if that went into the book I should have the fellows at Lord's coming to me in the pavilion and saying, "Look here, W.G., where did you get that word from?"'

About Dr. W. G. Grace there was something indefinable – like the simple faith of a child – which arrested and fascinated me. He was a big grown-up boy, just what a man who only lived when he was in the open air might be expected to be. A wonderful kindliness ran through his nature, mingling strangely with the arbitrary temper of a man who had been accustomed to be dominant over other men.

His temper was very fiery – perhaps gusty is a better word – and his prejudices ran away with him. He detested Radicals in politics, and disliked umpires who had ever given him out l.b.w. I asked him one day what he thought of a once famous Lancashire bowler, at that time ranking as a first class umpire. 'I don't want to say much about *him* in this book,' he replied. 'He gave me out l.b.w. to a ball that broke four inches when I was just "getting my eye in" at the Gentlemen *v.* Players match at the Oval in——' He could not forget that crowning offence. Of other men he had made idols – they could do no wrong. 'Ranji' was one of them. So were Charles B. Fry, F. S. Jackson and Archie MacLaren. We had warm arguments and all the little differences that collaboration almost necessarily involves; but never a moment of anger disturbed our relations, and we were good friends to the end of the partnership, and afterwards.

W. G. Grace would have made an excellent subject for a modern psycho-analyst who might, from W.G.'s subconscious stores of forgotten cricket lore, have extracted for us a classic of cricket literature. Reverting to W.G.'s choleric temperament, I think I once did make him really cross. It was when I flatly refused to believe his statement that he had only one lung, and had, in fact, had only one lung since his childhood. 'Now who,' I asked him incredulously, 'is going to believe that?' I simply could not credit it. Grace was, for the moment, nettled, and then he said rather testily, 'I'm not going to have you doubting what I say; I'll call my wife, and she'll confirm what I have told you.' He called Mrs. Grace, who corroborated W.G.'s story. Then I apologized and we made peace.

While I was engaged with Grace on his reminiscences and had about a third of the book written and revised, the publisher entered into an argument with Mr. W. M. Crook (now secretary of the Home Counties Liberal Federation and a great authority on London bird-life), who was then editing the *Echo*, for serial day by day publication of the chapters. I was horror-struck. I gravely doubted my capacity to keep up the regular supply of 'copy'; but serial publication was actually starting before I heard of the contract. The *Echo* got a fine fillip to its circulation from Grace's reminiscences. One day I was with my friend Mr. F. A. Atkins at the National Liberal Club when we met Mr. W. M. Crook in the hall. Mr. Atkins asked him if he was singing:

> Grace, 'tis a charming sound,
> Harmonious to the ear.

Mr. Crook smiled at the apposite quotation; but a few minutes later Mr. Atkins ejaculated: 'Why didn't I finish the quotation':

> Heaven with the Echo shall resound,
> And all the earth shall hear.

THE BEST I REMEMBER, *Cassell & Co. Ltd., 1922*

To W.G.
(by an old Admirer)

OH, W.G., tireless W.G.,
More power to your elbow! although one can see
Your foes hardly wished that at Brighton,
How many-at-forty could pile such a score?
But you, – may you do it a hundred times more,
My black-bearded cricketing Titan!

Two hundred and fifteen! Some thundering thumps
The ball must have had whilst you stood at the stumps
Till the trundles despaired at your wicket.
No woner they call you in jubilant glee,
and after another great W.G.
The very 'Grand Old Man' of Cricket. . .

The Cornstalks are rattlers, my William, all round;
As bowlers they're smart, and as batsmen they're sound
As good as they make 'em or pick 'em.
But, William, my champion, although we may feel
They're brothers in breed, foemen worthy our steel,
Our duty's to love, laud – *and* lick 'em!

Punch, 1888. After W.G.'s score of 215 against Sussex at Brighton

— 7 —

ANOTHER TALE OF THE TITAN

A 'W.G.' Story

MAJOR C. H. B. PRIDHAM

IN JUNE, 1886, W. G. Grace was down to play for the M.C.C. v. Oxford University. When it was first rumoured at Oxford that W.G. was going to play, his reputation was so great that the minds of several of the University eleven were filled with consternation. One of them said: 'W.G. is coming down to play for the M.C.C. and we shall never get him out. What can we do?' Another replied, and with some reason: 'We shall never get him out unless we can make him drunk'!! Due consideration had evidently not been taken into account that a bottle, or even two bottles, of champagne would have no more effect on his mighty frame than a liqueur glass of Kummel would have on a bunker on a golf course. However, J. H. Brain, who had played for Gloucestershire and knew the Champion well, generously decided to give a dinner party on the night of the first day's play; and every alluring arrangement was made to induce the strong personality of W.G. to fall to the general wishes of the undergraduates. Hopes ran high when the great man accepted the invitation.

It was June 21. Oxford won the toss, and, handicapped by the absence of several blues, who were in for schools, scored 142 runs. W. G. Grace and E. J. C. Studd then opened the innings for M.C.C. Those who had never before seen W.G. batting wondered, as he advanced towards the wicket, if he really was so wonderful a cricketer as he was said to be. His physique was splendid. He looked huge, and his large, dark beard gave him at first sight a dominating appearance, though possibly slightly lacking in agility on account of his size. Although his actual zenith had probably been ten years earlier, when he was slimmer and more active, he was not only champion in 1886, but he was universally recognized as such for many years to come.

He looked extremely bright and happy as he asked for guard and described a line on the ground parallel to the pitch with one of the bails. When facing the bowling his methods appeared to be simple. He gave a considerable uplift to his bat in a beeline from the bowler's arm to his wicket. The bowling obviously gave him no trouble, and it was delightful to see how, when playing back, he put such power into his strokes that, if the fielders failed to stop the ball it generally went to the boundary. The Parks' wicket was a lively one, and the most impressive part of his play was the way he treated the bumping balls. When a ball got up high on his off-stump or outside it, instead of leaving it alone he appeared to tap it down on the ground, generally to the boundary, as if he could place each delivery as he liked.

The opening pair were not out for 90 runs at the end of the first day's play, W.G.'s share of them being 50, made by what appeared to be faultless cricket. One who was there said that he was much struck by the charming manner with which W.G. treated the young men. He went out of his way to encourage and reassure all the keen young cricketers present. The dinner as a party was a great success. There was plenty of champagne going round, and all – including W.G. – thoroughly enjoyed the evening.

Next morning he went to the nets to have a few 'sighting shots' before continuing his innings. The number of those watching him was considerable, and all were full of interest. Now, there was a keen cricketer in his third year at Oxford who, incidentally, was playing for M.C.C. in this match. This was E. A. Nepean, who bowled what at first sight appeared to be simple deliveries, which, apart from an occasional slight off-break, turned very considerably from leg even on a fast wicket, when they came fast off the pitch. For some unexplained reason, Nepean's bowling was almost ridiculed until the following year, when he bowled for both Oxford and the Gentlemen v. Players at Lord's. On this occasion he was determined to bowl to the Champion at the nets, and actually clean bowled him with one of his leg breaks. This was really encouraging, and the fiction spread like wildfire: 'W.G. dined rather too well last night and can't see the ball at all this morning!' It was even asserted that he had been bowled out *three times* at the nets. When play began, however, it was soon obvious that no Oxford bowler was likely to get past W.G.'s bat. Centuries at that time were by no means common in the Parks, and when his score was 104 he was *given out l.b.w.* (modern critics of W.G. kindly note) to Page, the Oxford captain. He had hit fifteen fours and one six. The M.C.C. total score was 260.

Hopes were now centred on Oxford's second innings. Two freshmen with great public school reputations were being tried for the first time. The innings began to the bowling of W.G. and Walter Wright (the Kent professional), whilst M. C. Kemp kept wicket. W.G. actually secured *all ten wickets for 49 runs* (his analysis was: 36.2–17–49–10, overs of four balls), and he looked supremely happy, as he had every reason to be, when the M.C.C. won by an innings and 28 runs. During Oxford's first innings he was bowling when Hine Haycock caught a fine catch on the boundary at square-leg. During their second innings, when Brain looked like making many runs, he was brilliantly caught on the same boundary by the same fielder. W.G. remarked in high glee: 'I haven't had a man who could do it like that for me since poor old G.F.' G. F. Grace, his less famous younger brother, but a fine all-rounder, died in September, 1880, only three weeks after he had played for England v. Australia, at the Oval, together with both W. G. and E. M . Grace.

W.G.'s bowling on this occasion is thus described: 'With rather a low action, he seemed to put the ball towards the wicket rather than to bowl in the conventional manner.' It looked easy for a quick-footed batsman, but he did what he liked with the batsmen that day, and this was probably where the snare lay. W.G. was said at that time to be the best change bowler in England. Given a fast wicket, he probably required a full-sized ground even more than most slow bowlers. And although he might be hit hard and even frequently, his knowledge of the game and complete control of length enabled him to detect and attack any weak spot in the batsman's armour. He took* 2,876 wickets in first-class matches during his long career – a number only exceeded by six other bowlers in the history of the game, all of them professionals. In this particular match, the hospitable wiles of the undergraduates had conspicuously failed – in fact they had only succeeded in producing from the intended victim the almost unprecedented feat of a century and all ten wickets on the same day. The moral was that W.G. was impervious to the lures of a festive board.

The only other instances of a player taking all ten wickets as well as scoring a century are credited to V. E. Walker, for England v. Surrey, at the Oval, in 1859, and to W.G.'s elder brother, E. M. Grace for M.C.C. v. Gentlemen of Kent, at Canterbury, in 1862. E.M. scored 192, carrying his bat through the innings and taking fifteen wickets in a twelve-a-side match; with one man absent in the second innings he took the remaining ten wickets. It is interesting to note that, although thirty-eight instances have occurred since 1886 of a bowler taking all ten wickets in a first-class match, not one of the bowlers concerned has as yet equalled W.G.'s feat of scoring a century in the same match. Even in club cricket the double feat is extremely rare, but in 1929 R. G. Seldon, for Devon

*See Philip Bailey, p. 154.

Dumplings v. Somerset Stragglers in a two-day match at Exeter, took all ten wickets (hitting the stumps seven times) for 70 runs, and scored 100 not out on the same day.

To return to W.G. That night, after the game was over, another dinner party was given by another hospitable undergraduate – H. Acland Hood. One of the guests was a popular and well-known character at Oxford. When introduced to W.G., he asked: 'Did you see the cricket in the Parks to-day?' To which the reply was: 'Yes, I did.' The individual in question knew nothing about cricket, and had probably never heard of W. G. Grace – either as a cricketer or as anything else. At a time when W.G. was probably the best known and most easily recognized man in England, this, in itself, is a remarkable incident.

The recorder of the above story, Lord George Scott (who scored 100 for Oxford v. Cambridge in 1887 as a last choice to fill the vacancy caused by an injury to Wreford Brown, and whose average for Oxford v. Cambridge in three years, five innings, was 61), also gives the following details concerning W.G.'s hundredth century, in 1895: 'I had the impression that he considered his bat was to be used entirely as a weapon of offence. It was almost unknown for him to leave a ball alone. In 1895, when he was forty-seven years old and admittedly many years past his zenith on account of his great size and weight, he was nevertheless still the champion when conditions were easier for a batsman than they had been twenty years before. That year he played for Gloucestershire v. Somerset, at Bristol, on May 16, 17. On this occasion the Rev. A. P. Wickham was keeping wicket for Somerset, and W.G. scored 288 out of a total of 474 in 5 hours and 20 minutes, without making a single mistake. A. P. Wickham wrote to a friend afterwards as follows: "I had the advantage of watching that innings from the closest quarters, and have no hesitation in describing it as the most marvellous performance with the bat that I have ever seen. I can never forget the way Tyler's good length slows, converted by W.G. into half-volleys pitching about a foot outside the off-stump, were driven, rather than pulled, over mid-on's head, and pitched over the ropes. If these strokes had been counted as sixes (as they would now be), he would have nearly topped the 300. He only allowed *four balls* to pass his bat; one was on the leg-side and the other three were low ones on the off-side. But no matter how high the ball leaped – and Sammy Woods, who had forty overs at him, could 'prance' a bit – W.G.'s bat dropped on to them. Some of them went for fours, and others for a safe one or two to the man on the boundary, while those aimed at his head generally found the ropes on the leg-side!" '

Partly owing to his immensely powerful build, W.G. could stand great punishment when hit by fast bowling on his body. In 1896 he played in the opening match of an Australian tour for Lord Sheffield's eleven, at Sheffield Park, Brighton. The wicket was fiery, and E. Jones, one of the fastest bowlers of all time, hit him several times on the chest. A few days after this match W.G. showed his chest to a friend in the pavilion on the county ground at Bristol, who saw what looked like six or seven black puddings around his heart. W.G. said: 'Although I am forty-eight in a couple of months, I don't mind how fast they send them down to me. They can chuck them if they like; the faster they are the better. It's the slow ones I don't like. I never did. I know how they ought to be played, but I was never quick-footed enough to get bang out to them.'

It is probable that he derived his supreme batting efficiency from his remarkable physique and immense power, which in turn made it impossible for him to be quick-footed to the same degree as Jessop, who could dash into the middle of a cricket pitch to any ball. Nevertheless, W.G. was, as a batsman, far nearer perfection than any man in the Victorian era; and there has never been anybody in the same category against fast bowling, for in his zenith he was a terror to all fast bowlers, even on bumping wickets. W.G. was such a glorious figure on a cricket ground that when one arrived at Lord's and saw him at the wicket, it seemed almost too good to be true, especially when he proceeded to smite the ball in all directions. At the same time, when necessary, he could show wonderful and exceptional patience. Fifty years ago bearded cricketers were by no means uncommon, including such celebrities as Alfred Shaw, Barlow, Blackham, Boyle, Bonnor and others; but the beard of W.G. outshone those of all others by its voluminous magnificence. Many years ago, when the pavilion at Lord's was packed during the first day of a match between England and Australia, very many country members of the M.C.C. had come up full of interest to see this great match. Walter Forbes and my brother Henry were sitting in the pavilion watching the Australians batting, when a germ of mischief took possession of their brains. Henry, after looking at his match card, said: 'I think I can make out the names of most of the English eleven, but I wonder who that stout man with the large beard fielding at point is?' A man sitting immediately in front began visibly to fidget; so Walter Forbes said: 'I think that must be Abel.' The man in front could resist no longer, and turning round said: 'That, sir, is Doctor W. G. Grace.' Whilst thanking him for this valuable piece of information, Walter inwardly regretted that fat trout could seldom be induced to rise to his lures with such avidity.

These are a few instances connected with a man who for many years was magnificent, both in appearance and performance, on practically every well-known cricket ground in England and Australia. There are still some who played a great deal with him and know much more about his play than I do, but all agree that W. G. Grace was incontestably the champion of the game of cricket during the reign of Queen Victoria, and, taking into consideration the great number of wickets which fell to his bowling, there has surely never been one more deserving of the title, a fact which the late A. Stuart Wortley skilfully brought out in his masterpiece now hanging in the pavilion at Lord's.

THE CRICKETER, *July, 1942*

THE Hon. Alfred Lyttleton, the Middlesex and England wicketkeeper, claimed that W.G.'s was the dirtiest neck of any he had kept behind. W.G. seems not to have been particular about washing. Once on a tour of Australia in 1873 he was greeted by the proprietor of a shanty hotel: 'Pleased to meet yer, W.G., but we can't do you Sydney style, no bloody bathrooms and suchlike.' To which W.G. replied, 'That don't matter. We Graces ain't no bloody water-spaniels.'

WRITER'S CRITICISM

A God-send

CHARLES BOX

WHAT a God-send is Mr. W. G. Grace to the tribe of easy writers. Scarcely an incident in his life has been left unmentioned, to say nothing of the many which never occurred, except in the regions of romance and the fields of fancy. Stripped of the rhodomontade about his boyish feats, which were in accord with those of all the rest of his family, the first fact worth knowing is, that he came before a criticizing public at nearly the same age as Pilch, of whom Norfolk for many years proudly boasted. From the first blush of greatness which accompanied his *début* at Lord's in 1864, its lustre has never been dimmed. The heights he scaled have never been reached by any man since cricket was cultivated, and to what elevation he may hereafter aspire is beyond the ken of the most astute and the imagination of the most profound. His runs have been tabulated over and over again, and subjected to almost every process of arithmetic in order, if possible, to squeeze out some fresh wonder. Mr. Grace is certainly a prodigy of prodigies.

THE ENGLISH GAME OF CRICKET, The Field *office, 1877*

Captaincy

PELHAM WARNER

'W.G.' WAS not perhaps so good a Captain as one would expect from one who was so remarkable an exponent of the game, but it must be remembered that, in his day, the strategy and tactics of captaincy were not so much studied as they are now. Cricket, in a sense, was a more formal game. The field was set with, let us say, everybody on the off side, excepting a mid on, and if a batsman pulled a ball round on the leg side it was looked upon as almost a vulgar stroke.

I, myself, remember bowling for Rugby in the year 1889, in my first match for the School, and when the batsman, one of the New College, Oxford, XI, pulled me wide of mid on, as he ran up the wicket he apologized. I do not mean to infer that the cricketers in the days when 'W.G.' was playing did not pull or hook the ball, or take advantage of openings in the field, but what I do suggest is that batting was, generally speaking, more stereotyped in character, and as a consequence the placing of the field was a more formal affair.

MY CRICKETING LIFE, *Hodder & Stoughton, 1921*

Pitch Imperfect

E. H. B. SEWELL

THAT he was . . . something of an autocrat few would deny. None held more decided views than he, and he had a way with him that brooked no evasion on the part of others. An incident at a certain club game showed this. In order to make the most of his ground, he was obliged now and then to play more than one match on the same pitch. So it came to pass that a certain wicket on which two comparatively small scoring games had already been played was selected for a full day match. The visitors had their ground-man playing for them. W.G. won the toss. On reaching the pitch, the ground-man said to his captain loud enough for the Doctor to hear: 'Surely we ain't going to play on this wicket?' 'Why not?' rapped out W.G. at once. 'Why it's an old pitch. I s'pose it's some old dodge of yours,' replied the fellow very rudely. Grace wheeled round to walk to the pavilion and as he did so he thundered to the visiting captain: 'Unless that man apologizes, there'll be no match to-day,' and went on his way. The match was played and any one who knew W.G. can picture the delight with which he kept the visitors in the field until nearly five o'clock: 'just to show 'em there's nothin' much the matter with the wicket', as he put it. The biter generally was badly bitten when he tried to fix his teeth in the Doctor.

THE MEMORIAL BIOGRAPHY OF W. G. GRACE, *ed. Hawke, Harris and Gordon, Constable, 1919*

— 9 —

FROM GLOUCESTER TO LONDON

A Transfer of Allegiance

STEPHEN E. A. GREEN

IN 1899 the authorities of the Crystal Palace created a team which bore the name of London County Cricket Club and for the six years of its existence it had the redoubtable services of Dr. W. G. Grace as its manager, secretary and captain.

Each season the London County Cricket Club played various county sides, also the M.C.C. W. G. Grace recruited many famous cricketers for his side, including W. L. Murdoch, the former Australian captain. In addition club cricketers gained useful experience playing under the Champion. W.G. scored the last seven of his first-class hundreds for London County at the Crystal Palace, including 150 at the age of 54 against his native Gloucestershire.

The London County saga is, however, more memorable as being the origin of the final rift between Grace and the county club of which he was both founder member and leading light. It was Grace's intention to run London County and to be the Gloucestershire captain simultaneously. Although only 20 county championship matches were played at the end of the last century, Gloucestershire not surprisingly did not consider this to be a practical proposition.

Grace was in a sad predicament. In December 1898 he had lost his beloved daughter Bessie who had died of typhoid. One major reason why he agreed to accept the managership at the Crystal Palace was that he had given up his medical appointments in Bristol and had taken up residence in Sydenham. He hated leaving his wife at night and thus the need to take up a cricketing career in London was a very strong one.

The Gloucestershire Committee asked Grace at the beginning of the 1899 season to state exactly in how many matches he intended playing for his county during that summer. As Grace's biographer, A. A. Thomson, says 'this was both an ultimatum and an innuendo'. Neither was lost on W.G. Grace replied as follows:

St. Andrew's,
Lawrie Park Road,
Sydenham, S.E.
May 28th 1899

To the Committee of the Gloucestershire County Club

Gentlemen, in answer to yours of the 26th, re resolution passed on the 16th and kept back from me for reasons best known to yourselves, I beg to state that I had intended to play in nearly all our matches, but in consequence of the resolution passed and other actions of some of the Committee, I send in my resignation as captain, and must ask the Committee to choose the teams for further games as I shall not get them up.

I have always tried my very best to promote the interests of the Gloucestershire County Club, and it is with deep regret that I resign the captaincy. I have the greatest affection for the county of my birth, but for the Committee as a body, the greatest contempt.

I am,
Yours truly, W. G. Grace

The Committee thereupon passed a resolution which, in the circumstances, was fairly conciliatory:

'While the Committee are conscious of the great services rendered by Dr. Grace to the Gloucestershire Cricket Club as well as to cricket generally, and feel deep regret at his severance from them in spite of the efforts which have been made by them to avoid it, they feel they have no course open to them but to accept his resignation.'

Fortunately there was to be a happier ending to this melancholy saga. In 1902 Gloucestershire made W. G. Grace a life member of the club 'in recognition of his services' and in the same year fixtures between Gloucestershire and London County were arranged. To quote A. A. Thomson:

'In these two games the last breath of animosity was blown away. London County won both, one of them crushingly. W.G. must have chuckled good-naturedly in his beard over that.'

There are some other letters written from Sydenham by W. G. Grace which are preserved in the M.C.C. Library. Whilst they are not of the same importance as the one addressed to the Gloucestershire Committee, they do show W.G. to have been a conscientious – if laconic – letter writer.

On 20 August 1900 he wrote to Lord Harris:

'I presented the pads to the M.C.C. some years ago but they did not seem to appreciate them. I have never seen them since the new pavilion was built, I should know them again if I saw them. They might be just away with a lot of rubbish or they might be destroyed. I will enquire about this when I go up to Lord's which will not be until after Hastings. I saw you were knocking them about again the other day. My back tendon on the right leg is sprained a bit so that I cannot get between the wickets very fast or I should have made 150 the other day.'

On 27 October 1903 the most famous cricketer in the world found time to write as follows to F. B. Wilson of Trinity College:

'Just a line to congratulate you on your appointment as Captain of the University for 1904. I trust you will be able to get a good team to uphold the honour of Cambridge Cricket, especially in the inter-varsity contest.'

Grace could be generous as a cricketer but economical in other ways, as is confirmed in two letters which he wrote to F. S. Ashley-Cooper the 'Herodotus of cricket'.

On 25 October 1907 he told Ashley-Cooper 'I bowled in several matches when I did not bat, as I gave our men an innings, who sometimes, owing to heavy scoring, did not have a chance of batting.' On 3 April 1907 he told the same correspondent 'By some reason that is unknown to me, I have not received *Cricket* for now nearly two years. I thought the reason was that Alcock had given it up. Perhaps you will see I am again put on the free list.'

Grace wrote quite a few letters to the industrious Ashley-Cooper. On 3 July 1908 for instance, W.G. told him (he was in his 60th year!) 'I took 7 wickets and scored 111 not out. My youngest son C. B. Grace scored 68 and we put on 100 runs in the hour when in together. My son also scored 128 on June 24th for old and present students of the Engineering

School at the Crystal Palace.' Grace was always very proud of the achievements of his family.

On 13 December 1908 he summarized his achievements that season to Ashley-Cooper: 'I should have scored 1000 runs only I injured my foot at Lord's on August 19 and played only twice or three times afterwards.'

In the M.C.C. Library there are other letters which Grace wrote from his Sydenham address to correspondents as diverse as G. R. Merrick, a 'former brother officer under the poor law in Bristol' and J. A. Lester, the famous American cricketer. Perhaps enough has been quoted already, however, to catch the flavour of one of the most famous inhabitants of South East London at the turn of the century.

TRANSACTIONS, *Lewisham History Society, London Borough of Lewisham , 1973*

IN A match during which W.G.'s brother E.M. appealed frequently but to no avail, W.G., as yet another appeal was turned down, said confidentially to the umpire, 'Never mind my brother, he's always appealing. Now when I appeal it *is* out.'

W.G. and his New Work

by THE EDITOR *of the Captain*

I SEIZED the terra-cotta envelope, and drew forth the message it contained.

'*Can see you to-day.*' In five minutes I was hurrying down Burleigh Street. Arrived in the Strand I leapt into a cab and drove to London Bridge Station. Through fog and gloom into sunlight I travelled, for the pall which hung over central London could not reach as far as Sydenham, where the Crystal Palace is, and where the London County Cricket Club has its headquarters.

I paced along a quiet street or two, and then turned into Lawrie Park Road, where, at a house called 'St. Andrew's', I found Dr. Grace – a burly, genial giant, whose bulk makes his activity a matter of wonder – a giant in a wholesome woollen waistcoat, and dark grey tweeds.

Dr. Grace was up to his neck in documents, for as all the cricket world must know by this time, he has given up his medical practice at Bristol to act as secretary and general manager to the club which has been christened 'The London County Cricket Club'. This is why the doctor's desk is littered with notepaper and envelopes; this is why the morning, afternoon, evening, and late-night postmen fill the doctor's letter-box with a never-ending supply of cricketing correspondence. But he loves not pen or ink, and so he arose and shook himself like a St. Bernard dog, put on a square felt hat and a black overcoat, and led me away in the direction of the Crystal Palace grounds, talking gruffly, but good-temperedly, and with no little enthusiasm, about the new venture of which he is the head, the middle, and the tail.

'A good many people,' I observed, 'have only a faint idea as to what the London County Club is, and as to what it is going to do.'

'I'll tell you,' said the doctor. 'There are in London two great cricket grounds – the Oval and Lord's. Now, it has struck the Crystal Palace directors that this South-Easterly part of London is badly off for cricket. It is quite a little journey from here to Lord's or to the Oval (although, of course, a man who wants to watch good cricket doesn't mind how far he travels, so long as he knows that an excellent game at his journey's end will reward him for his trouble), so the London Country Cricket Club has been formed to provide first-class cricket, not only for the tremendous population of this district, but for the hundreds of thousands of people who want to follow their favourite pastime, and, at the same time, breathe this lovely Sydenham air. Here we are, practically in the country, although within five-and-twenty minutes' ride of town.'

At this juncture we arrived at a side entrance to the Palace grounds: the doctor opened the door with his private key. A few steps and a short walk brought us to a little park, where numbers of men were busy levelling and turfing, and building the new pavilion, which, I may mention, is to cost over £3,000.

In the old pavilion we found Murch (the bowler), who is head of the ground staff of the new club. I cast my eyes round the extraordinary structure which, for so many years, has done duty as a pavilion. The doctor observed that it was more like a chapel, and I fully agreed with him.

As we strolled on I could not but observe how concentrated was the doctor's attention upon everything appertaining to and affecting in any way the ground upon which the new team of Australians will make its *début*. Mossy turf is bad for cricket. The doctor pointed out to me the places where moss unfortunately makes its appearance – nowhere near the centre of the arena, however. He explained that the mossy growth had been caused by the rain running down the slope from the path above. Some branches of the trees at the Palace side appeared to overhang the ground a trifle too much. Not much – but the doctor's hawk-like eye espied them, and he promptly gave orders that the ends of those branches were to be ruthlessly executed. Underneath the trees are seats – these will be the spots most affected by shade-lovers when the summer sun is hot.

'We can seat five thousand spectators,' the doctor said.

We walked on, and surveyed the wide, green ground from every point of view. Now I am an Englishman, and, as such, I like my beef and beer – or their equivalents, according to the occasion. I therefore suggested to the doctor that it would be a good plan to have little hand wagons (similar to those you see at railway stations) to be wheeled round the ground, so that cricket watchers may get a cup of tea and a bath bun without having to scramble for such commodities in front of the counter.

'Refreshments, sir,' replied the doctor, discreetly, 'are not in my department. We have an excellent caterer.'

I said I would send the caterer a marked copy of *The Captain*.

Then I got on to another topic.

'Will schoolboys and 'Varsity men be allowed to join the L.C.C.C. during the vacation at reduced terms?'

'Yes,' was the answer, 'on payment of two guineas instead of three. All members have to be proposed and seconded before they can be put up for election.'

I made a careful entry in my notebook to this effect, and then:—

'As touching the fair sex, doctor?'

W.G. stroked his beard sagaciously.

'I think all members,' said he, 'will have the privilege of taking ladies and friends, without payment, into the members' enclosure, except on certain big match days, when they will be charged admission. It is not customary on any ground to admit ladies to the pavillion.'

'To continue my catechism, doctor——.'

He shuddered.

'To continue my catechism,' I went on, in a hard voice, 'am I to understand that one gains an advantage over later joiners by being elected on or before May the First?'

'Quite so,' said he. 'The Annual Subscription is three guineas for playing members, and two guineas for non-playing members, both inclusive of season tickets to the Crystal Palace. The entrance fee is two guineas, but all members joining before the First of May are exempt from entrance fee.'

'What are some of the best fixtures you have booked so far?' demanded the man from Burleigh Street.

'We lead off with a good one – SOUTH OF ENGLAND *v.* AUSTRALIANS, on May 8th, 9th, and 10th. I am getting a strong SOUTH side together. The match *v.* OXFORD UNIVERSITY will be a good one, and against WORCESTER-SHIRE – the new first-class county. A "promoted" county's work, during its first year of promotion, always excites a lot of interest. We also play the M.C.C. and other counties and clubs of all sorts.'

'Any public school matches?'

'Cheltenham *v.* Haileybury on August 3rd and 4th.'

'You think the ground will be big enough for them?'

'Considering' said the doctor, 'that the ground is 230 yds. by 170 yds. – one of the best grounds in the kingdom – I think,' he added, reflectively, 'that it'll be big enough for the Cheltenham and Haileybury boys to play on.'

Rambling round, although the doctor wanted to talk about nothing else but the L.C.C.C., I deftly succeeded in making W.G. tell me something of his early cricket days. (By the way, he won a hurdle race at the Crystal Palace when he was five-and-twenty or so. And, talking about jumping, reminds me of a story in which W.G.'s jumping proved very helpful to the police. . . .)

According to Mr. Methven Brownlee, Dr. Grace's old friend, and a man to whom the world is indebted for a quantity of delightfully-told personal information about the great cricketer, W.G. was in the zenith of his cross-country powers about 1870. He succumbed to E.M. in the hop, step, and jump, however.

Well, W.G. got out at a wayside Gloucestershire station one day, and found that a lady had given a man into custody for picking her pocket of a purse containing 50s. The prisoner was big and slippery, and the constable something of a greenhorn, the result being that the purse-snatcher glided out of his grasp and bolted away across the neighbour-ing meadows. To place a whole field between himself and his astonished custodian was the work of a couple of minutes. W.G. came up at this moment, and, sympathizing either with the lady or the representative of the law, or perhaps both, he dashed off in pursuit. By this time the alleged thief was blundering through the hedge of the next field, and, though W.G. had won many a hurdle race after being heavily handicapped, there seemed little prospect of his landing his man after giving him such a start. Bounding over the fences, however, as though he thoroughly enjoyed the 'sport', he soon lessened the distance between himself and the accused, and, settling down to the work with the pluck for which he is noted, W.G. rather astonished his man by the quickness with which he placed himself in uncomfortable proximity to him. While the pursued was struggling and blundering through the hedges, W.G. cleared the obstacles at a bound, and a Gloucestershire policeman described him as taking a formidable-looking iron gate with the ease and confidence with which he would clear a hurdle. In this way, after a good spin – rather beyond his usual 'distance' – the pursuer headed his man, who, having no wish to cultivate a closer acquaintance with the square-built, muscular form of the redoubtable athlete, doubled back, and was ultimately run into the arms of the policeman (who had joined in the pursuit) and locked up in safe custody.

That little sprint in the cause of justice was taken almost twenty-six years ago. Henceforth that Gloucestershire district which W.G. loves so well will know him not, save when he travels down to Bristol to play against the county which he captained for so many seasons. The doctor has plunged heart and soul into his new work; he never does anything by halves, and the London County Cricket Club will be a success because the man who is the prime mover in the new concern does not know how to spell the word 'failure'. He is being assisted by a very able executive committee, on which one finds such well-known and responsible men as Sir Richard Webster, Sir Arthur Sullivan, and Mr. A. J. Webbe. I never met a more enthusiastic man on cricket than the Middlesex captain.

The intention is to offer every possible inducement to cricketers to join the club, rather than to make it a mere medium for attracting the outside public to the Palace. Good ground bowlers will officiate at the nets – and this fact should be well digested by those who intend to join the club, for really good cricket practice at all reasonable hours in London is not easy to get. Dr. Grace will make it his aim to ensure this.

Talking of these and other matters concerning the L.C.C.C., we found ourselves at the pleasant side-gate again. On the way back to 'St. Andrew's' I asked the doctor what he thought was the best thing to keep one'e eye in for cricket, and he replied that, from observation and from what his own sons say, 'fives' is the best game for keeping one in practice, and especially so in the case of schoolboys. W.G. thinks that any exercise is good so long as it keeps all the muscles in working order. Personally, he finds that running with the beagles is excellent training for wind and limb.

With reference to the somewhat uncertain train service to the Crystal Palace, W.G. is in hopes that a good deal of this will shortly be altered, for he informed me that it has been promised from a very reliable source, and that steps will ere long be taken to have the train service greatly re-organized.

Referring to his visit to America in 1872, W.G. told me that he found the summer heat of New York very trying, but that the most comfortable place for spending the day was the cricket-field, the atmosphere not being so humid there as in town. Canada the doctor found very pleasant, the weather being more like an English summer.

When asked what he thought about baseball, he replied, with a smile: 'I am no judge. Base-ball is one thing and cricket is another.'

Dr. Grace is not a one-sport man; he is an 'all-rounder', if ever there was one. He is a splendid shot and a very fine whist-player, and I may add that he weighs 18st.

Dr. Grace is, indeed, a grand type of the dogged Englishman – the sort of Englishman that causes his country to be held in profound respect by the whole world. He always goes on – he fights on whether his sun of prosperity is shining or whether misfortune has dealt him a hard blow. This is the type which all boys should endeavour to emulate, for here, in this famous cricketer, you have a happy combination of sound brain, sound heart, courage, perseverance, and muscle. Season after season 'the old man' (as you often hear people call him) has come up, bat in hand, and held his own with fellow-cricketers in the prime of athletic life and trained to the hour.

Yet, in spite of these formidable competitors, year after year Dr. Grace has laid down his bat in September with a thousand runs, made in first-class cricket, booked to his credit.

Folks have said: 'You see; Grace will retire at the end of this season!'

Not a bit of it; the first week in May you hear somebody say at breakfast: 'Hullo! W.G. made a hundred yesterday!'

Grace has been idolized by the English speaking world. Royalty has shaken him by the hand and sent him letters of congratulation; magazines and newspapers the globe over have printed countless pages and columns about him; yet he is absolutely unspoiled by success. A little off-hand and gruff he may be occasionally to persons who force themselves upon him – but such persons merit a cooler reception than even he gives them. At Lord's and the Oval you may see people, on the drawing of stumps, rush right across the ground and hail the doctor as if he were a next-door neighbour of theirs. Hero-worship is all very well, but it should not be carried to this extent. Besides, the doctor is of a singularly retiring disposition. Imagine the money he might have made in this country and America by lecturing on the game of which he is the finest exponent ever known; yet, until quite recently, each winter has found him busily attending to his medical duties, physicking the poor of Bristol – in his capacity of parish doctor – and (as he has always done) making the most of every hour in his day. Grace is a man who has never wasted time. When you come to realize what a short thing life is, it is appalling to think what a lot of it some people waste – or to what an unprofitable use they put it. 'All work' is bad, and 'all play' is bad – an agreeable mixture of both (and plenty of both) is the ideal life.

Dr. Grace is close on fifty-one, hale and hearty, a long way from being 'out' yet. In this, the first magazine article to describe his change of occupation, we wish him all the good luck and prosperity his enterprise and energy should win him.

THE CAPTAIN, *1899*

London County

COLONEL IAN MAXWELL CAMPBELL

To MANY of us the year 1898 is memorable in cricket annals, for it brought Dr. W. G. Grace to Sydenham as Secretary and Manager of a club newly formed by the Crystal Palace Directorate and called London County Cricket Club. Of the original conception and the intentions behind it I know little or nothing. There was considerable and outspoken opposition on the part of members of our old and well-established Crystal Palace Cricket Club to this unexpected intrusion and to their being taken over lock, stock and barrel by the new concern. We have become accustomed in recent years to possessive aggressions, both internal and international, but in those days they were uncommon and deeply resented. A temporary compromise had to be arranged whereby both clubs played their own matches during the season of 1899 and issued their own lists of averages at the end of it when the old club was 'faded out'. In one or two of the new club's matches, the better ones, its team was simply called W. G. Grace's XI. I played in one against Oxford University. By the following year the amalgamation and reorganization were complete, and London County Cricket Club was recognized as 'first class' in its matches against Surrey, Worcestershire, Derbyshire, Warwickshire, M.C.C. and the two Universities: all its other matches were excluded from first-class status. I shall always nurse a little feeling of pride in the remembrance that in the last two years of the old Crystal Palace Cricket Club's existence I headed the batting averages, though I took rather a lowly place in those of the bowlers. I cannot help thinking that W.G. himself helped the decline in my bowling: he would be continually urging me to 'give them that ball of yours that nips off the pitch so quickly', and I think I unconsciously began to pay more attention to 'nip' than to pitch, pace and break . . .

The first fairly important match in which I played for the new London County in 1899 was at Swindon *versus* Wiltshire. W.G. had collected a strong side which included W. Troup, W. S. A. Brown and C. L.

Townsend, all of them, like himself, from Gloucestershire. Charlie Townsend, most loosely built bowler one could imagine but full of wiles, together with the Doctor and my old school-fellow L. S. Wells, a good all round cricketer and elder brother of C.M., diddled Wiltshire out and left us only 90 runs to get to win in the second innings. I use the word 'diddled' there in its appropriate and most respectable sense and primarily because all our three bowlers were slow and two of them of the spinner and googly type, to risk introducing anachronisms. Two fine cricketers, O. G. Radcliffe and Awdry Miller, were playing for Wiltshire and tried valiantly to avoid defeat.

I cull this 'wee modest crimson-tippèd flow'r' from an occasional diary: – 'I shall not forget in a hurry a compliment W.G. paid me indirectly when, in speaking to my father after the Wiltshire match, he said "your son is a beautiful fielder". I would rather "fielder" there than "batter," "bowler", "fellow" or anything else except perhaps "orator". As I shall never get that I am contented with "fielder".'

REMINISCENCES OF A VINTER, *Chapman & Hall, 1950*

AT LUNCHEON I sat next a boy whose father had played for Gloucestershire. He told me of the fact and afterwards I introduced him to W.G. 'Very glad to make your acquaintance,' said the Old Man, 'and I hope you're a better fielder than your father was. He was the worst that ever I did see.'

— 10 —

I RECALL HOW . . .

Two Remember

PERCY GALE AND GEORGE BELDAM

Percy G. Gale writes:

'IF MY friendship with W. G. Grace began late in life, it became a warm one. In fact the inner group of the London County Club was like a happy family. Grace himself was known as Father, W. L. Murdoch as Muvver, "Livey" Walker as the Babe and I as Granny – why I was given that nickname I do not remember, unless it was because I was slow in the field. I never played a first-class match until I was thirty-seven and my only prolonged season was then, in 1900. But I played a rare lot of club cricket with W.G., and invariably he showed the same tremendous relish for the game, always extremely kind to younger players, himself rather like a big rollicking lovable boy – in fact it was love he inspired amongst those often with him.

No story about W.G. is so well known as his writing to Phil May to know why in a caricature he had sketched short-leg wearing gloves, and the artist replying on a post-card "to keep his hands warm." But here is a sequel: I have myself played in a cricket-match with W.G. in the present century in which he actually fielded at point wearing wicket-keeping-gloves for precisely the same purpose.

I once ran W.G. out very badly when I was his partner. I would have given the world to have crossed him after my call, but could not do it. He was very angry at my getting him out, and he told me so pretty forcibly when I soon followed him compulsorily to the pavilion. But fury was soon spent with the dear old man, and not a quarter of an hour afterwards, his big hand was laid on my shoulder as he invited me "to come and have a whisky." I remember running Murdoch out just as

Whatever her musical accomplishments, Martha Pocock, W.G.'s mother, gave the world a gift from the Gods (*MCC Library*)

It is doubtful if young William Gilbert could remember much of the interior of Downend House. He moved with his family to The Chestnuts when he was only two (*MCC library*)

Kempt and studious. Aged about 22 (*Roger Mann Collection*)

In a Bath back garden. Aged
25 (*MCC Library*)

The West Gloucestershire team at Knowle Park, Almondsbury. *Back row* (L to R): Rev. H.W. Barber, H.M. Grace
(father of W.G.), H. Gruning (black beard), A. Pocock (uncle of W.G.). *Middle row*: W.G., Henry Grace, E.M.
Grace, Alfred Grace (a brotherly quartet). *Front row*: F. Baker, W.J. Pocock, G.F. Grace (the youngest brother), R.
Brotherhood (appropriately named!) (*Roger Mann Collection*)

The English Gentlemen Cricketers in America, 1872.

ABOVE R.A. Fitzgerald's team. *Back row* (L to R): A. Lubbock, W.G., T.C. Patteston of the Toronto Club, C.J. Ottoway. *Middle row*; E. Lubbock. R.A. Fitzgerald, A. Appleby. *Front row*: F.P.U. Pickering, Hon. G. Harris, A.N. Hornby, W.M. Rose, C.K. Francis (*Roger Mann Collection*)

A rather self-conscious pose for the camera. Slim and serious (*Roger Mann Collection*)

Articles of Agreement

made and entered into this   day of September 1873 Between William Gilbert Grace of Downend in the County of Gloucester Gentleman of the one part and   of   in the County of   Cricketer (hereinafter called the said Cricketer) of the other part Witnesseth that the said William Gilbert Grace hereby engages the said   to proceed to Australasia to play in 14 Cricket matches ~~of three days each~~ at such times and places as the said William Gilbert Grace shall from time to time direct for a period extending over about 100 days and returning on or about the 25th day of March 1874 And in consideration thereof the said William Gilbert Grace hereby agrees to pay the said James Lillywhite the sum of £150 at the times and in manner hereinafter mentioned; and the said J. Lillywhite hereby agrees to and accepts the said engagement upon the following conditions that is to say

1. The said Cricketer is to report himself to the said William Gilbert Grace at Southampton on the 22nd day of October 1873 to embark on board the Peninsular and Oriental Steamer bound for Australia and announced to depart on the 23rd day of October 1873

2. The said Cricketer hereby agrees during such period as aforesaid to place himself under the entire disposal and directions of the said William Gilbert Grace and to obey all his orders and to play in each of the aforesaid 14 Cricket matches if required by the said William Gilbert Grace so to do And the said Cricketer hereby agrees with the said William Gilbert Grace that he will not play in any other Cricket match or Cricket matches than those authorized by the said William Gilbert Grace or engage in any other pursuit without the consent in writing of the said William Gilbert Grace first obtained ~~until the fourteen matches have been played~~

3. The said William Gilbert Grace hereby agrees to provide for the said Cricketer a free second class passage to Australia and back to England by one of the Peninsular and Oriental Steam Company's Vessels and to provide Hotel accommodation and to pay all travelling and other expences during the said engagement except wines spirits and other liquors but hereby agreed to pay the said Cricketer the sum of £20 ~~towards his expences~~ for wines spirits and other liquors

4. The said sums of £150 and £20 to be paid as follows £150 on the said Cricketer ~~embarking at~~ Southampton ~~aforesaid~~ ~~ready to embark~~ and a further sum of £50 by ~~his equal~~

'All right then, don't smile . . .' (MCC Library)

The tour agreement between Grace and James Lillywhite. The Sussex professional was paid £150 plus £20 spending money for the trip to Australia, 1873/4 (*Roger Mann Collection*)

OPPOSITE LEFT Sir Leslie Ward's Spy Cartoon. In *Vanity Fair*, June 1877 (*Burlington Gallery*)

OPPOSITE RIGHT The Souvenir of Grace's Testimonial was sold with the *Cricket and Football Times*. The £1,500 raised enabled the Doctor to buy a practice at Stapleton Road in Bristol (*Roger Mann Collection*)

The United South of England team at Priory Park, Chichester, 1874 (*Roger Mann Collection*)

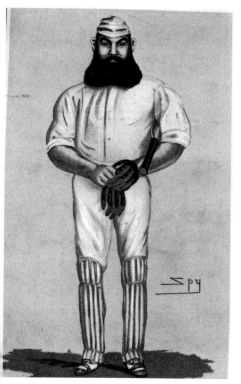

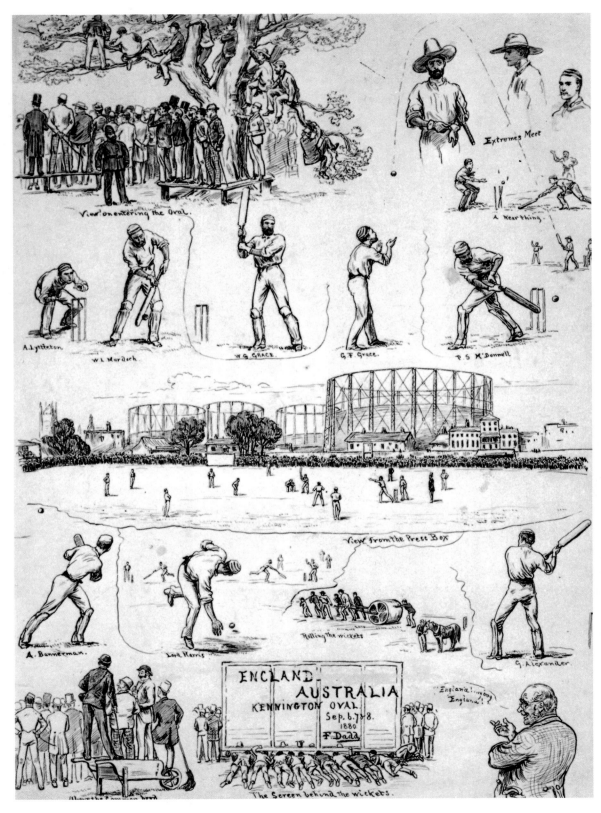

Dadd's composite drawing of what is regarded as the first Test Match ever staged in England. The home side won by five wickets and Grace scored 152 in the first innings (*MCC Library*)

Crayon and wash drawing, Alfred Bryan
(*MCC Library*)

A lithograph by an unidentified artist, *c.* 1880s, that used to
have pride of place in the saloon bar of The Yorker public
house in Piccadilly, London. Recently sold by the Burlington
Gallery to a collector in the USA (*Burlington Gallery*)

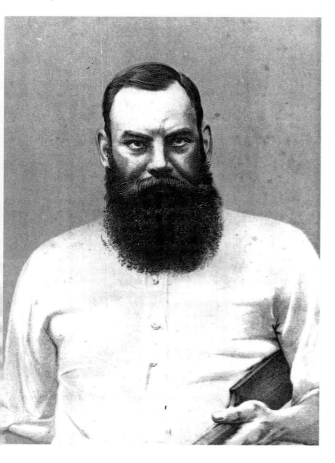

Lithograph by A. Spalding (*Roger Mann Collection*)

The Captains of the County Cricket Clubs of England for 1886

W.G. between strokes. Cartoons by Harry Furniss from *A Century of Grace* (*MCC Library*)

The two Test Captains, W.L. Murdoch and W.G, (*Roger Mann Collection*)

With David Munro at the Mid-Surrey Golf Club, September 1893. Captioned 'The Heavenly Twins' (*MCC Library*)

At the head of the
troops. A *Punch*
cartoon (*MCC Library*)

LORD'S IN DANGER.   THE M. C. C. GO OUT TO MEET THE ENEMY.

["Sir EDWARD WATKIN proposes to construct a Railway passing through Lord's Cricket Ground."]

In 1891 by Act of Parliament the Manchester, Sheffield & Lincolnshire Railway
were authorised to build tunnels from Marylebone Station running under the
Eastern fringe of Lord's Cricket Ground. This proposal had been strongly
opposed by the M.C.C., but finally the matter was settled by the M.C.C. giving
up part of the freehold of the Practice Ground in exchange for a larger area
occupied by the Clergy Orphans School on the condition that the Club were
granted a ninety-nine year lease of the ground immediately over the tunnels.

A festive occasion with the Gloucestershire players. Possibly at Bristol in 1895 (*Roger Mann Collection*)

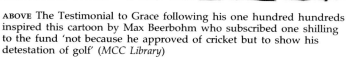

ABOVE The Testimonial to Grace following his one hundred hundreds inspired this cartoon by Max Beerbohm who subscribed one shilling to the fund 'not because he approved of cricket but to show his detestation of golf' (*MCC Library*)

ABOVE, RIGHT A watercolour produced in 1895 by Cecil Cutler who lived in Putney. Could have been a commission by the I. Zingari Club whose blazer Grace is wearing together with his favourite MCC cap (*Burlington Gallery*)

Doulton ewer *c.* 1895, 7¼'' high. George Giffen, K.S. Ranjitsinhji and W.G. adorn with each portrait contained within a medallion having a decorative border (*Burlington Gallery*)

A Coalport dessert dish in rococo design celebrating Grace's century of centuries. Possibly produced for the Centenary dinner (*Burlington Gallery*)

A printed cotton handkerchief, 23½'' by 24'', manufactured in 1895, detailing the hundred hundreds (*Burlington Gallery*)

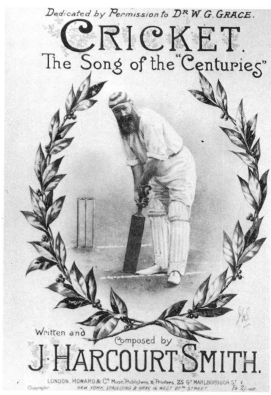

Composers and publishers were not slow to cash in on a national figure.

BELOW A metal figure on a raised wooden platform with the two arms and the bat moving on a spring (*Burlington Gallery*)

Carved wood pipe. The stem is in the form of a bat. Inscribed 'W.G.G. Aet 47'. 1895 Centuplico (*Burlington Gallery*)

A Butler bronze (*Roger Mann Collection*)

Wood carvings by Anton Wagner (*Roger Mann Collection*)

At various ages in various materials including plaster, biscuit and parian ware by Robinson and Leadbetter

FAR LEFT (*Roger Mann Collection*)
LEFT (*Burlington Gallery*)
OPPOSITE, ABOVE LEFT (*MCC Library*)
OPPOSITE, ABOVE RIGHT (*Burlington Gallery*)

Pen and ink Jubilee sketches. Likely to be by the nineteenth-century illustrator Charles Slocombe (*Burlington Gallery*)

Gloucestershire 1898. *Back row* (L to R): Smith (scorer),
Murch, Hale, Wrathall, Brown. *Middle row*: Roberts,
Townsend, W.G., Troup, Jessop. *Front row*: Board,
Goodwin, Sewell (*Roger Mann Collection*)

Pushing the sightscreen at Trent Bridge, July 1898 in
preparation for practice prior to the match, Notts *v.* Gloucs
(*Roger Mann Collection*)

badly, but, as he passed me on the way to the tent, all he said was, "Now you've to make a century just because I cannot." He did not mind for even the space of an instant.

Once W.G. was the victim of a small boy. It was at Chesterfield and he had something on a race and wanted to know the result. He and I were walking inside the ropes during the match when a boy shouted "Special". "Here you are," said W.G., giving him twopence. I noticed the boy made a precipitate bolt. On opening the paper, Grace found it was the advertisement sheet of a morning half-penny issue.

I was always struck with the fatherly way W.G. looked after his people. There can be no harm now in saying that at times the authorities at the Crystal Palace found difficulty in meeting their financial obligations, so every Saturday morning Grace made a point of going to see that his groundsmen were duly paid. Dyer, the pavilion attendant at the Palace, was a quaint individual. Once I asked W.G. why he had brought him from Bristol. "Well it was this way," replied the Old Man in his characteristic fashion; "when I was leaving for the Crystal Palace, Dyer told me he had had a dream that I was taking him with me, so of course he had to come. And when I was moving to Eltham, he said to me that it was an odd thing but he had had another dream that he was going to be my gardener, and so it had to be, of course." I saw Dyer on a mourning coach at the great man's funeral.

W.G. had a jolly way of proclaiming what was to be done. In Cyphers *v.* London County, he said, "Come along, Granny, we've both to make hundreds," and we did. On this occasion he went in pretty late.

Every one will truly tell you W.G. never played for his averages, but here is a burlesque incident to prove the contrary. It was in this century and the last match of the season. I perpetrated the fact that in club cricket Murdoch averaged 70 and Poidevin 99. "And what do I average?" asked Grace. If you made 86 not out to-day, you would average 100, was my reply. "Very good," he ejaculated into his beard. He proceeded to bat admirably and when his own score was 86, declared the innings closed. "Must beat those boys once more," was his chuckling comment. This is the only time I ever heard him refer to his own average.

The last time he and Spofforth ever met in a match was L.C.C. *v.* Hampstead. Each bowled the other out and curiously enough each of them took no other wickets in the innings.

Once, at Sutton, W.G. declared and lost the match. He had fifteen catches missed off his own bowling. He stood watching misses at last with an expression almost of amusement on his face. At length he dropped one himself. "Missing catches seems catching," he grumbled as he picked up the ball.

He had a masterful way with him at need. I recollected a batsman disputing an l.b.w. decision on an appeal W.G. made off his own bowling. The champion raised his head and thundered: "Pavilion you." Those two words were enough. The batsman retired instantly.

On Victoria Day, I recollect our team singing "God Save the Queen" in the field, W.G. conducting by waving a stump. He made top score on that occasion – remembering all his career, one is almost tempted to add, as usual.'

G. W. Beldam, as thoughtful in criticism as at cricket, golf or photography, writes:

'I WELL remember my first meeting with W.G., the idol of every one's boyhood. I had been fairly successful for some years as a club cricketer and my friends were even keener than I was myself that I should come into first-class cricket; but for some three years before W.G. came to London or even thought of doing so, I had a strong presentiment that if I came into first-class cricket it would be through knowing W.G. For some time after London County Cricket Club was founded I preferred to play for my old clubs, but one day in the Oval pavilion I was introduced to W.G. by D. L. A. Jephson and it seemed to me I had known him a long time. Thus commenced an acquaintance which became one of close personal intimacy.

In the first matches I soon saw what a great and genuine desire he had to be of real assistance to aspirants for first-class cricket, and how naturally and quickly he made excuses for any failure where he saw he was dealing with "triers"; but there was no doubt about his attitude towards "slackers", and because of this those who knew him only by name, were apt to misjudge his attitude in this respect. There never was any man more ready to make an excuse or to sympathize with failure or more keenly joyful at the success of those playing under him than the dear Old Man. To play under him was to worship him, so that he drew out the highest effort. To know him was to love him.

I remember in the match London County v. Wiltshire being fearfully bewildered at something he did. He was standing point and twice appealed for "leg before wicket" from that position. Having only just come to know him I did not like even to mention it to any one, but I remember it struck me as very extraordinary that he, with such a knowledge of the game, should appeal from a position in which it was evident that he could only be approximately sure that the ball had pitched in a line between the wickets.

In the pavilion he gave me the opportunity which I hardly expected. When Wiltshire were in the field he turned to me and said: "I say,

George, that chap fielding point isn't much good, is he?" I said: "Do you mean because he doesn't appeal for leg before wicket, Doctor?" Then I thought I had gone too far, but my doubts were immediately dispelled by him coming for me, laughing all over his face and chasing me round the table.

The only time I ever remember him even looking angry for the moment with me, was when he was bowling, and I was put in the long field. The ball was skied and dropped about fifteen yards over mid-on's head. I started to run from long-on and then seeing I could not possibly get to it, was hoping to get the batsmen to run two, with a chance of a "run-out." Then I heard: "Come to her, George, come to her." They ran two and the "run-out" nearly came off, but W.G. was too intent on his own idea that I ought to have attempted the catch. I remember saying: "Look here, Doctor, I can't do the hundred in five seconds!" and heard some mumbled words from him. He may have been right, but I didn't think he was.'

THE MEMORIAL BIOGRAPHY OF W. G. GRACE, *ed. Hawke, Harris and Gordon, Constable, 1919*

A Memory

ARTHUR CONAN DOYLE

TO THOSE who knew W. G. Grace he was more than a great cricketer. He had many of the characteristics of a great man. There was a masterful generosity and a large direct simplicity and frankness which, combined with his huge frame, swarthy features, bushy beard, and a somewhat lumbering carriage, made an impression which could never be forgotten. In spite of his giant West-of-England build, there was, as it seemed to me, something of the gipsy in his colouring, his vitality, and his quick dark eyes with their wary expression. The bright yellow and red cap which he loved to wear added to this Zingari effect. His elder brother, the Coroner, small, wizened, dark, and wiry, had even more of this gipsy appearance. I speak, of course, only of the effect produced, for I have no reason to think that such blood was in his veins, though, following Borrow, I am ready to believe that there is no better in Europe.

There was a fine open-air breeziness of manner about the man which made his company a delight and added a zest to the game. He was, of course, a highly educated surgeon, but he had rather the fashion of talk which one would associate with a jovial farmer. His voice was high-pitched, considering the huge chest from which it came, and it preserved something of the Western burr. 'Hullo, young 'un, a bit too good for you, that one!' 'Never mind, my lad, you're not the first good man that has dropped an easy catch.' 'Shut your legs to it before you try to pick it up.' These were the scraps of advice or consolation which he would shout – the voice was loud though high – to the youngster who needed admonition or sympathy.

His style and methods were peculiar to himself. In his youth, when he was tall, slim, and agile, he must have been as ideal in his form as in his results. But as this generation knew him he had run to great size and a certain awkwardness of build. It was amazing that a man who was capable of such exertions should carry such weight. As he came towards the wicket, walking heavily with shoulders rounded, his great girth outlined by his coloured sash, one would have imagined that his day was passed. 'He may make his twenty or thirty,' one thought, 'and then Nature will dismiss him if the bowler fails.' Never was there a greater fallacy. He seemed slow, stiff, and heavy at first. When he had made fifty in his quiet, methodical fashion, he was somewhat younger and fresher. At the end of a century he had not turned a hair, and was watching the ball with as clear an eye as in the first over. Younger batsmen might tire and grow ragged in their strokes, but never the old man. It was his advice to play every ball as if it were the first — and he lived up to it. There was no feeling for the ball, no half hits or wild slogs. Everything that he did was firm, definite, and well within his strength. I have had the privilege of fielding at point more than once while he made his hundred, and have in my mind a clear impression of his methods. I do not know if he took the centre or the leg guard, or the point between them, but he actually stood very clear of his wicket, bending his huge shoulders and presenting a very broad face of the bat towards the bowler. Then as he saw the latter advance he would slowly raise himself to his height and draw back the blade of his bat, while his left toe would go upwards until only the heel of that foot remained upon the ground. He gauged the pitch of the ball in an instant, and if it were doubtful played back rather than forward. Often he smothered a really dangerous length ball by a curious half-cock stroke to which he was partial. He took no risks, and in playing forward trailed the bottom of his bat along the grass as it advanced so as to guard against the shooter – a relic no doubt of his early days in the 'sixties, when shooters were seen more often than on modern grounds.

The great strength of his batting was upon the offside. I should not suppose that there was ever a batsman who was so good at controlling that most uncontrollable of all balls, the good-length ball outside the off stump. He would not disregard it, as is the modern habit. It was, indeed, seldom that he let a ball pass without offering at it. He did not flinch from it as a foe, but rather welcomed it as a friend, and stepping across the wicket while bending his great shoulders he watched it closely as it rose, and patted it with an easy tap through the slips. In vain with a fast bumpy bowler pounding them down did three quivering fieldsmen crouch in the slips, their hands outstretched and eager for the coming catch. Never with the edge of the bat, but always with the true centre, would he turn the ball groundwards, so that it flashed down and then fizzed off between the grasping hands, flying with its own momentum to the boundary. With incredible accuracy he would place it according to the fields, curving it off squarely if third man were not in his place or tapping it almost straight down upon the ground if short-slip were standing wide of the wicket. In no shot was he so supremely excellent, and, like all great things, it seemed simplicity itself as he did it. Only when one saw other great batsmen fail did one realize how accurate was the timing and the wristwork of the old man. When he was well on towards his sixtieth year I have seen him standing up to Lockwood when man after man was helpless at the other wicket, tapping those terrific expresses away through the slips with the easy sureness with which one would bounce a tennis ball with a racket. Nor was he ever to be frightened by the most dangerous bowler. Poised and firm, he never flinched, but turned the rising ball to leg or patted it to the off. The fastest bowler in England sent one like a cannon-shot through his beard, with only a comic shake of the head and a good-humoured growl in reply.

It was in this command of the off ball and in his perfect defence that his great merit lay, but there was no stroke at which he was not adept. With his true eye he hit a larger proportion of leg balls than any other man. He stepped back and struck them off his legs not with a whole-hearted swing, but with a sharp, decisive turn of the wrists, watching the ball to the last instant. The only shot which he produced less frequently than his contemporaries was the big sixer, beloved of the crowd. He seldom ventured that great effort, which has an equal chance of ending on the pavilion or in the hands of cover-point. His batting was always well within his strength, and though an analysis of his scores will show that he found the boundary as often as anyone, he never gave the impression that he was hitting hard.

I think that when he was well set the best chance of getting rid of him may have been to serve him up with something so delectable that he might be tempted into a liberty. This theory occurred to me after watching him play seven professional bowlers of all paces and types until he had topped the hundred. Since the best had failed, I thought I would try the other variety – I was captaining an M.C.C. team upon that day – so I ventured upon an experimental over. It succeeded to a marvel. A half volley upon the off with all the fielders upon the off side tempted him to sweep it round to the on. For once he got it on the edge and it went an amazing height perpendicularly into the air, and then down into the hands of Storer, the Derbyshire wicket-keeper. The old man laughed and shook his head at me. He was thinking probably that it was the worst ball that ever got his wicket, but he was too polite to say so. He was not always polite, however. I can remember that in the second innings of the same match he was given out leg-before to Cranfield, a left-handed bowler, bowling round the wicket. I forget who the umpire was, but the old man was very angry. I can see him now with his thick, padded, and somewhat bandy legs, marching towards the pavilion, but his face and beard turned over his right shoulder while he glared back and rumbled all sorts of comminations. His temper grew somewhat shorter, I fancy, during his latter days. It is not surprising when one considers the strain of a succession of three-day matches upon a man of his age. At his normal he was a cheery, boyish-hearted, and boisterous man, the jolliest of playmates.

Of his bowling I have very clear recollections. He was an innovator among bowlers, for he really invented the leg theory a generation before it was rediscovered and practised by Vine, Armstrong, and others. Grace's traps at leg were proverbial in the 'seventies. His manner was peculiar. He would lumber up to the wicket and toss up the ball in a take-it-or-leave-it style, as if he cared little whether it pitched between the wickets or in the next parish. As a matter of fact this careless attitude covered a very remarkable accuracy. His command of length was absolute, and he had just enough leg spin to beat the bat if you played forward to the pitch of the ball. He was full of guile, and the bad ball which was worth four to you was sent, as likely as not, to unsettle you and lead you on. Never shall I forget three successive balls which I received from him, the graduated stages of a trap which was my undoing and my ruin. The first was a dropping half-volley which no one could help hitting for four. The next looked exactly the same, and I had pranced out to it before I realized that it was really somewhat shorter. I hit at it none the less, and with some luck and a sidelong shot scored another four. The third seemed far the most tempting of the three. No child could have lobbed up anything more seductive. Only when I was ten feet down the pitch did I realize the effect was produced by a higher trajectory, and that the ball was really so short that I could not get at the pitch of it. It shot past me with a little top spin to put devil into it, and I heard the squawk of 'How's that?' as Lilley put down my wicket. There was the old man rubbing his great brown hands and wagging his beard in laughter as I marched sadly home to the dressing-room.

Those who knew him will never look at the classic swL of Lord's without an occasional vision of the great cricketer. One can see him in many typical attitudes. Most clearly perhaps he appears coming down the pavilion steps, with ten thousand people clapping as the red and yellow cap, the huge stooping shoulders, and the famous black beard emerge from the open door. Very clearly also can one recall him when he was dissatisfied with the wicket and had detected some danger spot which the roller had missed. He would squat out on the pitch, sitting on his heels and slapping away with his bat to flatten out the trouble. Most clearly of all, however, one sees his big figure in the centre of an after-luncheon group, and as one approaches one hears again that jolly voice and roar of infectious laughter. He was and will remain the very impersonation of cricket, redolent of fresh air, of good humour, of conflict without malice, of chivalrous strife, of keenness for victory by fair means and utter detestation of all that were foul. Few men have done more for the generation in which he lived, and his influence was none the less because it was a spontaneous and utterly unconscious one.

THE STRAND MAGAZINE, *1927*

WILLIAM HEMINGWAY was often to be found in the dressing-room with his back to the window reading Greek. When Hemingway on one occasion complained to W.G. about his own temporary lack of success, the Old Man replied: 'How can you expect to make runs when you are always reading? I am never caught that way.'

The Big Break

F. R. SPOFFORTH

[In] his recollections of Grace, F. R. Spofforth writes:

[One] time I met him was in that famous one-day match at Lord's. The curious thing was that though the Club's first total was only 33, yet there was a change, because I was put on in place of Allan because he was bowling so badly, though he got Grace's wicket. We knew nothing of the English climate then and fielded shivering in silk shirts, not one of the team having a sweater.

The figures Sir Home Gordon has shown me of what Grace did in matches against me, 37 innings, 1,042 runs, 28·16 average, considerably less than his general average, bears out my theory that I never had any particular difficulty in getting him out. I clean bowled him seven times. A. C. M. Croome says that W.G. told him that on any wicket he never knew when I should bowl him. This may have been due in part of my artfulness. I always had a silly mid-on for him and that invariably worried him. I used to put my fingers round the ball in odd ways when bowling to W.G., just because I knew he watched my hand so closely. Once he hit a single off what was merely a long hop, and when he came to my end he asked, 'What were you trying to do with that ball?' I had not been trying anything except to lull him into inattention, but I replied: 'You are the luckiest bat in the world; it's just my bad luck that I did not get on a big break from the off and send you back.' The very next ball he had from me, he was ready for me to try that big break. I knew he would be, I was sure his great leg would come in front to allow him to reach the ball. So I sent a perfectly straight one dead at the leg-stump, which hit him hard on the pad. 'How's that?' 'Out,' said Luke Greenwood, and as W.G. walked back, grumbling and growling, he added: 'I can't help it; no, not if you was the Prince of Wales hisself.'

THE MEMORIAL BIOGRAPHY OF W. G. GRACE, *ed. Hawke, Harris and Gordon, Constable, 1919*

MY 'W.G.'

by A. E. Lawton

Foreword JACK HOBBS

IT was for Surrey against the Gentlemen of England that I made what was called my debut in first class cricket. Included amongst the opposition was A. E. Lawton and first impressions being the most lasting ones, I shall never forget how much I was encouraged in that game by the author of this book.

By those words of encouragement – who can tell – he may have made a whole world of difference to my cricket life.

The friendship thus started explains why I am particularly happy – even proud – of the opportunity – to write the foreword of this book. That same match brought me into first real contact with W. G. Grace – the greatest personality I have ever met on the cricket field. Vividly the memories of that great player come back to me. I remember him getting his hundredth century at least as clearly as I recall the struggle I had to register the century which took me past the 'W.G.' record. Seldom are we able to resist the temptation to make comparisons, but between the old-timers and the moderns there cannot be any worthwhile comparison. Times have changed. There may never be a greater run-getting machine than Don Bradman. There will certainly never be a greater cricketing personality than 'W.G.'. He left his stamp on the game to an unequalled degree. Some of us will, of necessity, receive occasional mention in the years to come, because our names are here and there in the reference and record books. But we shan't be remembered down the years as 'W.G.' is remembered. As they speak of him his contemporaries reveal how they love his memory, and they pass on the memories in a way which keep the Old Man 'alive'.

This book about the greatest personality which our glorious game, studded with personalities, has ever known, will be welcomed by many thousands.

It is a long time since I read a book with so much compelling interest. I could not part company with the pages until I reached the end, and believe me it is a very good book on cricket which has that effect.

Jack Hobbs, 20 August 1947

PREFACE

AT the outset I would like to state that in setting down these experiences I have referred to no old Score Cards nor have I refreshed my memory by even one single glance at any WISDEN. All the details are still fresh in my mind. I mention these facts so that a reader may the better appreciate how permanently the personality, the character and the unstinting friendliness of an outstanding sportsman may be embossed for always on a humble devotee who gratefully offers these recordings as a tribute.

A. E. Lawton

FIRST of all let me explain how Cricket came into my life. My earliest recollection is of a sheepdog – our old family pet – who, after being missing for two days, was found dead in the middle of the cricket pitch at Dukinfield where I was born. I was five years old at the time and the loss of 'Laddie' marked my first encounter with Tragedy. I was taken to the ground, probably as some form of consolation, to watch a Cricket match being played. So there and then I suppose the germ entered into my soul. Believe me, it is still there.

A dozen years elapsed before I was taken to Old Trafford, as a tremendous treat, to watch a Lancashire v. Gloucestershire match because the famous Dr. Grace was playing. I didn't see him bat on that occasion but I was much impressed by his burly figure and that long black beard he wore. That day I heard his stentorian voice. An unusual incident had occurred; the pitch was on the soft side. A. C. MacLaren, wearing his Harrow Cap, was batting; he stepped back, forced a straight ball well wide of short leg – called out 'come two' to his partner, and started to run. Then came the outburst from Dr. Grace. 'You're out, Archie (he pronounced it almost like Aerchie), you're out.' He repeated this several times while the batsmen ran their two runs. Dr. Grace pointed to the stumps at MacLaren's end and said 'You trod on your wicket'. Sure enough the leg bail was on the grass. I couldn't hear MacLaren's reply, but I remember being tremendously astonished at his 'standing up' to Dr. Grace. It seemed like sacrilege to me just then. However, on being appealed to, the umpire decided that MacLaren had completed his stroke before he commenced to run and therefore he was 'not out'. MacLaren continued his innings whilst Dr. Grace tugged away at his beard and gesticulated for quite a while afterwards.

The day came when Dr. Grace loomed somewhat more intimately over my horizon – he had become my cricket hero from the moment I discarded weekly periodicals such as 'Comic Cuts' and 'Ally Sloper' for daily newspapers with their accounts of County Cricket, Gentlemen v. Players and North v. South cricket matches. The great occasion was when a Testimonial Fund was being raised for a presentation to Dr. W. G. Grace and my father asked me if I would like to make my contribution. Pocket money was small in those days – it was a shilling fund – but I was awfully proud to send in my shilling and to see my name in the newspaper – I think it was the *London Daily Telegraph* – a few days later. I don't remember the total amount subscribed, but my recollection is that it was well over a thousand pounds, which marked a considerable sum in those days.

What was 'W.G.' like to look at at close quarters? Well I would say well over six feet tall – I wouldn't call him exactly burly, I think lumbering expresses my meaning more clearly. It was in 1900 that I first met him – that would be when he was nearly 52 years old. A healthy florid complexion surrounded by his ten inch black beard. A pair of eyes humorous and shrewd. A deep penetrating but by no means unpleasing voice. . . .

When he bowled he paddled up to the wicket one, two, three, four, five, six, seven steps and then sent along a lobbing ball with a very slightly above round arm action, which made it somewhat difficult to gauge just where the ball would pitch. When he turned it, it was only a matter of three or four inches.

Came 1900 and my introduction into first class county cricket. After a dismal failure in my first match which was against Lancashire at Old Trafford – and I had been specially coached for three weeks by Mold and Briggs – I was dropped and then given another chance. Fortune was now on my side, I became a regular member of the Derbyshire eleven and in due course we had to go to a beautiful ground to play against the Club which W. G. Grace had just founded under the name of the London County Cricket Club at the Crystal Palace. L. G. Wright – our No. 1 batsman – conducted me to the Amateurs' dressing room and I was half way into my flannels when the door opened and in walked Dr. W. G. Grace himself – he was already changed. 'Hello, Wright, how are you? Glad to see you again' (they had played together in several Gentlemen v. Players matches at the Oval) boomed my hero. Then L. G. Wright after a sentence or two said 'W.G. this is our new recruit, A. E. Lawton'. Out came a huge hand to fairly wrap itself round mine – and mine is by no means small – accompanied by a hearty 'How d'ye do, *I've heard of you!*' Try as I will I can never recall my reply. *He'd* heard of *me*! As I say I don't know how I answered the great man and to this day I don't know how I ought to have replied. But from that moment I knew I would do anything for him. Such can be the force of personal magnetism.

During my first match against W. G. Grace's London County Eleven I made 23 and 37 and did some fairly good scouting in the long field. When the match was over 'W.G.' – yes, it was really 'W.G.' by then – took me on one side and said he wanted me to join his London County Cricket Club, finishing up with: 'You see your father when you get home and tell him I want you to play in all our matches when you have no Derbyshire fixture on – and tell him I'd like him to join too'. The upshot was that when I retold the conversation to my father he replied at once:- 'All right my boy, of course you must join and I'll join too. From this moment we go into partnership together, you and I, I'll make the money and you'll spend it.' That, incidentally, is just about what happened. Can you blame me? I was only 21.

In that first match at the Crystal Palace the Derbyshire Captain, S. H. Evershed put me on to bowl. 'W.G.' had to take my first ball in first class cricket. Evershed asked me what field I wanted – I was fast medium – and I had the usual field, two slips and so forth. I sent down the first ball dead on off stump, quite a good length, but 'W.G.' promptly clouted it good and hard to the long-on boundary. Exactly the same thing happened the next two balls and my captain from midoff remarked to me 'I don't think you know where you want your fielders, do you?' 'I don't think I do', I replied ruefully. The next ball I sent down as fast as ever I could – W.G. just blocked it and called out: 'Well bowled youngster. That was a pretty good 'un, Evershed.' A couple more overs were enough to show my skipper that I didn't stand an earthly of breaking the partnership. So I didn't get 'W.G.'s' wicket – then.

'W.G.' took me with the London County side to Cambridge to play against the 'Varsity. We won the match by five or six wickets. I didn't get many runs but I made the winning hit. I was in with 'W.G.' at the time. He made no attempt to score after I joined him at the wicket. I was content to keep my end up while he got the necessary runs, but that didn't suit him. He wanted *me* to get them and, particularly, he wanted *me* to make the winning hit. This I didn't learn until afterwards, but his 'Well played, Bertie' as we were returning to the pavilion was made as encouragingly as if I had scorerd a century. A kindly soul? I'll say he was! My contribution was sixteen or so.

What sort of a doctor was 'W.G.'? I can't say positively; I always understood he was a general practitioner. I often saw him tend cuts and rapped fingers, but of my own experience of his medical hints I can only pass on one or two pieces of advice. When he saw me bathing my tired and slightly sore feet after a whole day in the long field he told me that if I wore *two* pairs of thick socks, I would never be bothered again with either trouble. I took his tip and soon proved that 'W.G.' knew what he was talking about. Also he told me that there were two medical points to bear in mind – 'You will find – playing County Cricket – that one may sometimes get constipated, at other times, the – er – the other way about. So when you get constipated a little whisky and ginger ale will quickly and quietly put you right. If you find yourself – er – the other way about – take a brandy and port, you'll see that will do the trick.' Dear old 'W.G.', he was right, both innings.

I have often thought that the reason I got on so well with 'W.G.' was because I never dropped a catch off his bowling – and I took quite a few. His 'field' always included two deep square legs, right on the boundary, one on either side of the umpire. Directly he went on to bowl I invariably went to the forward side of the umpire and 'W.G.' would amble up to the wickets and with his round arm action toss up his 'donkey-drops' either on or just outside the leg stump. Very tempting to the batsman who sooner or later would proceed to sky one in our direction, mainly in mine. Just before the end of my first season I was amazed but genuinely thrilled to receive a telegram reading, 'Will you play for North versus South at Lords on August 31st and following days (signed) GRACE, HAWKE'. I replied that I would be delighted and then telegraphed to my father for permission. That came along all right.

In that match I first met A. E. Stoddart, D. L. A. Jephson and G. L. Jessop. 'W.G.' got a wonderful century the first innings and I was busy chasing the ball at deep third man and in the long field. At the start of the South second innings Lord Hawke elected to open the bowling from the pavilion end with Ernest Smith, the Yorkshire amateur fast bowler. To my surprise he sent me to field at short slip. I took up what I thought the correct position but Lord Hawke said, Oh no, he wanted the slips three yards closer up. The opening pair were again Stoddart and 'W.G.'. In the fourth over 'W.G.' cut hard down a rising fast one from Ernest Smith – I flung out my right hand and managed to catch it six inches from the ground. 'W.G.' looked at me and said 'All right, young man, that's the last time you'll be asked to play by me' – and then he called out to Stoddart 'That's the fellow *I* got on the side and look what he does to me'. Oddly enough I managed to catch Stoddart at short slip soon afterwards. Mark you I was very young and was a bit uneasy when I returned to the dressing room at the end of the match. 'W.G.' came up to me with a slip of paper in his hand saying 'Well caught, Bertie – here fill up this paper. I will be the seconder – I never propose anyone, but I'll get someone who will.' He got the Notts. President, W. E. Denison. The paper was a nomination for Membership of the M.C.C. And he got me elected a few months later.

At the beginning of 1901 season 'W.G.' wrote asking me to come to London a few days before Easter and get some practice at the Crystal Palace nets, as then I should be fit for the London County Match against Surrey at the Oval. This match for some years was a standing dish for Easter Monday, Tuesday and Wednesday. In one of them we had to stop play three times for *snow*! One member of our side was L. O. S. Poidevin the Australian batsman who had qualified for Lancashire. He was a little late in arriving on the first day. 'W.G.' had lost the toss and we were out in the field when Poidevin trotted down the steps. Great Scot, how fat that little fellow had grown during the winter! We made comments to 'W.G.' on those lines – he said nothing but how his eyes twinkled in that ruddy face – his beard was showing streaks of grey now. Presently he put Poidevin on to bowl his slow leg breaks. Poidevin set his fields long off, long on, deep square leg and so on and then proceeded to take off his sweater. His sweater indeed; he peeled off one, he peeled off a second, then a waistcoat which still left him wearing *two* sweaters in which he bowled. Then we realized that 'Poidy' hadn't gained weight; neither had 'W.G.' lost his spirit of mischief.

One September I was invited by W. Smith, the Oxfordshire cricketer and Oxford City football captain, to play for Witney in their Annual Feast matches. 'W.G.' had played for some years in the Witney Feast games and so had G. L. Jessop. Jessop couldn't turn up so would I take his place? Would I take the chance of staying in the same house as 'W.G.'? I'll say I would and did. The family made blankets so we were sure of warm beds. The cricket was quite serious but the fun we had afterwards! Following dinner all in the Billiard Room where we watched Mr. William Smith, Senior, and 'W.G.' play a game of billiards. Both were nothing out of the ordinary but both tried hard to win. I never saw two players pot their opponents ball so often – or so deliberately. One evening we went down to the green where John Ball the old prize-fighter was running a variety show in a tent. He also had one of the very earliest film cameras and had taken some pictures of our match two days before. That night we actually saw ourselves on the screen – in action – many years before cinemas were built. I was sitting next to

'W.G.'. At the interval that remarkable man handed me a cap he had 'borrowed' from the Smith household and said, 'Put this on, pull it well over your eyes, now turn up your coat collar' – the he unbuttoned his coat, pulled out a dinner plate, also abstracted from the house, and continued, 'Now go round, gruff your voice, *and collect for the attendants.*' I told you before that I would do anything for him so I did what he asked me and collected eight or nine shillings in coppers. John Ball fairly bellowed with laughter when I took the money to him and explained the prank of 'W.G.'. The cap, by the bye, belonged to another son of the house, Herbert Smith, the Reading captain and left full back, with twenty International Caps to his name.

When the 1902 season started 'W.G.' staged his opening of the Season at the Crystal Palace with his London County side against the very powerful all star Australian eleven captained by Joe Darling and including Victor Trumper, Reg Duff, Clem Hill, Monty Noble, Albert Cotter, Hugh Trumble and Warwick Armstrong. 'W.G.' didn't play – it was long afterwards that I learned he had stood down to give *me* a chance! Archie MacLaren was our skipper and we had C. B. Fry, Walter Brearley, G. L. Jessop and such like. The newspapers said that I was the only player in the team that had not been considered as a Test Match possible. I happened to get top score and the Press put it down to the fact that the probables were most likely over anxious. But 'W.G.' was delighted at my success, so was Archie MacLaren for he promoted me from No. 8 in the first innings to No. 4 in the second. I only made 16 and while Victor Trumper was catching me at third man, mid-on was dodging my bat which had slipped out of my hands! A few days before this Australian Match 'W.G.' had had me down at the nets for a few practice knocks and then gave me a one day match. 'Nothing like a bit of a loosening up, my boy, and then a bit of match practice.' Now in this practice match we had a newcomer who had just joined the London County Club. After tossing the coin on the grass in front of the pavilion 'W.G.' came back into the dressing-room with, 'Well, boys, we've won the toss and we're batting – Murch (the old Gloster professional) bring me an order form.' This being at once forthcoming 'W.G.' wrote down:- (1) W. G. Grace, (2) W. L. Murdoch, (3) G. W. Beldam, paused and looked round the room. His eye caught sight of the young recruit and he said in his kindly way – 'Look here, young fellow, where do *you* generally go in to bat.' The newcomer, rather taken aback, replied, 'Oh, anywhere, Dr. Grace, anywhere at all,' – then, with an impulsive burst of confidence, 'I can tell you I have never made a duck in my life.' Quick as lightning, as he stroked his wise old beard, came 'W.G.'s' retort, 'Then you haven't played much cricket. You go in No. 11' – and number 11 he went in. . . .

I think it was that year, when I was playing at the Crystal Palace in a one-day match against, I believe, Beckenham, that some wag pulled a good one on 'W.G.' and got us all shrieking with laughter. 'W.G.' had lost the toss and we had to field. He decided to open the bowling himself from the scoreboard end. As he was walking back for his short run a youngster ran out from the scoreboard gesticulating wildly. 'W.G.' waited until the boy came quite close and then asked him what he wanted. It was only this: 'Bowler's name, please'.

'W.G.' was a great advocate of having a bit of a knock at the nets before the commencement of play every day, even up to his last match, and we all got the same habit, those of us who played with him. I don't see so much of that nowadays, more's the pity, *I* think.

I don't ever remember 'W.G.' having a bet on a horse, though when playing at Cambridge once he did introduce me to Dick Marsh who was King Edward's trainer. Yet 'W.G.' had an occasional bet – always for the same amount – and never more than one with the same individual. He would choose his time to just after a wicket had fallen. This is how he worked it on me. He took me to one end, handed me the ball and said 'You can bowl one ball – only one, mind, and I'll bet you a shilling you don't hit the stumps at the other end'. I tried, I bowled a straight one – but it went over the top – so I lost my bob. Cute old 'W.G.'. It needed a straight yorker or full toss, but I didn't think about that until too late.

Did you ever hear that 'W.G.' could blush, even when well over 50 years old? Well, I saw him do so and this is how it came about. When first class teams go a-visiting county cricket grounds the local theatre managers usually send complimentary tickets along. Well, at Birmingham, while 'W.G.' was batting a man came up to me in the pavilion and asked if I was not one of Dr. Grace's cricketers. I replied in the affirmative and he said he was the manager of the theatre where Weedon Grossmith was playing in *The night of the party*, and Mr. Grossmith would be very glad to hold a box at the disposal of Dr. Grace that evening. I took it upon myself to say that he could count upon some of us bringing 'W.G.' along. He handed me the box ticket before he left. Driving back to the Hotel in an open fourwheeler I told 'W.G.' I wanted to take him to the theatre, but he flatly said it was nothing in his line. I added that I had secured tickets, and he retorted that I had more money than sense. Then I explained that Weedon Grossmith was particularly keen on cricket, that the manager had come down specially to Edgbaston and I produced the ticket for the box and said I had promised to take him. Well, if I'd promised he supposed he had to go. We went. Do you remember the plot? The owners of the house go out for the evening and the servants take advantage of their absence to have a Party. Covers are taken off the drawing-room furniture and there is high revel until they hear the owner (Weedon Grossmith) returning most unexpectedly. Back go the covers and all leave the drawing room, undiscovered, except the exceedingly pretty parlourmaid who flings herself on the settee and has just flung the cover over it and herself when in comes Weedon Grossmith, who proceeds to seat himself on the settee. Got that? Right. At the interval we are invited to go down to Grossmith's dressing room to have a glass of champagne. We went. 'W.G.' was in great form and was saying that, although he was enjoying the show immensely, he would have liked it even more if he could have sat on that very pretty young lady. At that very moment the lady herself came and Weedon Grossmith, with his delicious laugh said 'I'm sure you would – let me introduce you to the lady – my wife – Dr. Grace'. Oh yes, 'W.G.' blushed all right – and for quite a while.

I have tried to make it abundantly clear that at all times I received from 'W.G.' every kindness, every consideration and all sorts of helpful advice and encouragement as did many other young cricketers – and naturally I resented any remarks made against him. Always he was keen and he certainly liked his own way. But who doesn't? Don't forget that he was twenty-five to thirty years older than many great England cricketers, with and against whom he played. He was born at Thornbury in Gloucestershire and occasionally I heard the remark 'Thornbury Rules'. Maybe the term originated through a tale of 'W.G.' being clean bowled first ball in a match and, placing the bails back on the stumps, he calmly went on to bat after remarking – that was a 'trial ball'. And at one time in the long ago the first ball was a trial ball. But when Derbyshire played one season at the Crystal Palace 'W.G.' opened the London County innings with about three-quarters of an hour to play. For some reason only one recognized first class umpire turned up and one of the ground staff was co-opted. I put my fast bowlers on – Joe Humphries was keeping wicket, Charles Ollivierre, the West Indian player, was at short slip and Bill Storer – a former England wicketkeeper – at second slip. When 'W.G.' was about a dozen he tipped one into the hands of Humphries who was standing back. There was, of course, the usual general appeal and to our utter amazement the 'local' umpire said 'NOT OUT'. Then Storer butted in with 'Well caught, Joe', at which 'W.G.' burst out with 'You've no business to say that, Storer'. During the last over of the day he again quite palpably tipped a ball into Humphries' safe hands – the same umpire again gave him 'Not Out'. Came the climax about the fourth over next morning when again 'W.G.' edged another fast one. This time the catch went to Ollivierre who took it about six inches from the ground, at the same time yelling, 'For goodness sake don't appeal, anybody'. 'W.G.' just gave him a glare and then walked back to the pavilion.

I well remember a match at Chesterfield against London County. 'W.G.' lost the toss and we put up a fair score. The weather was showery and the attendance not too good. On the second day we had to wait quite a while for the pitch to dry. When a start was made we had a big crowd of miners who turned up knowing they would see 'W. G. Grace' go into bat. He took an amateur – P. G. Gale in with him. As always, when I have seen him, 'W.G.' took the first ball. He hit it a little wide of cover, called 'No, yes, go on' as he saw it going to extra cover and ran down the wicket. But Gale turned back to his own crease with 'I'm not coming, Doctor'. 'W.G.' continued down the pitch yelling, 'Well, don't run me out.' Gale regained his crease, the ball was returned to the wicketkeeper's end and Humphries had no difficulty in taking it and the 'Old Man' was run out first ball. Had it not been for those incidents at the Crystal Palace when 'W.G.' was twice given 'Not Out' I think Humphries would have let the ball go through his hands and let the crowd have another chance of watching the great man. As it was many of the spectators left at once. 'W.G.' was peeved all through the match. When I went in to bat he went on to bowl and I was content to place him for twos and singles. After a bit he called out to me 'If you don't hit 'em I shall go off'. So I thought it would serve him right – and suit the crowd – if I proceeded to collect a few 'sixes'. Up came the half volley just outside the leg stump and I gave it what it wanted. It was a beautiful shot but Gale, fielding at my old place on the square leg boundary ran six yards and not only stopped it from going over the ropes but made a really brilliant catch. So he and 'W.G.' were friends again. But 'W.G.' did not altogether recover his wonted geniality. There was no chance of a finish but I went on to the field and said to 'W.G.': 'If I declare will you yourself go in for the hour remaining for play?' But he declined firmly so the match just petered out. That was the only time I ever remember seeing 'W.G.' out of temper.

That grievances can stick in certain minds even in the great game of cricket is well illustrated in the following story. The scene was Derby – I think it was 1900. 'W.G.' came in to bat first on a soft wicket. I want to lay especial emphasis on the fact that the pitch was soft. Bill Bestwick was the bowler – old Mordecai Sherwin the umpire at the bowler's end. The very first ball pitched nearly a foot outside the off stump – 'W.G.' moved across to play but it broke back just enough to beat the bat and struck 'W.G.' on the pad. Bestwick made what was only a half hearted sort of involuntary appeal. Without hesitation up went Sherwin's hand and 'W.G.' was given out L.B.W. Off he went, of course, and we all got in line with the two lots of stump and could see without a shadow of doubt where that ball had pitched. 'W.G.' had not been out by a good eight inches. (In those days a ball had to pitch straight to obtain a legitimate L.B.W. decision.) I remember S. Hill-Wood turning to ask Bill Chatterton – who was our oldest professional – why Sherwin had given 'W.G.' out. And I remember Chatterton's brief but expressive reply *Old wounds*. I can't help laughing every time I call the incident to mind because Chatterton pronounced the word 'wounds' to rhyme with *bounds*. I have often wondered just what started the ill feeling but I never found out. Sherwin was many years before my time and I didn't come across him afterwards. Somehow I forgot to sound 'W.G.' about it.

On three occasions playing at the Crystal Palace I have seen 'W.G.' throw a cricket ball hard from one hand to the other – you know how the umpire chucks the ball to the team as they come out to field – a brand new one, of course – and then not only refuse to play with it, but he each time made his groundsman Bill Murch saw the ball in half. On every occasion 'W.G.' was right – the core was wood instead of cork!

Another time I played with Derbyshire against 'W.G.' and his London County side at the Crystal Palace – his main bowlers were Cranfield the Somerset left-hander and Len Braund the famous Somerset and England all-rounder. When I had met Braund before he had been a fast bowler with three and sometimes four slips, but by now he had changed to bowling slow medium leg breaks with an occasional very fast one. 'W.G.' to my surprise put Cranfield at 'Silly-point' for me and Braund was bowling. I thought it was a joke and asked 'W.G.' if he really meant Cranfield to stand so close in. 'Are you all right, Cranfield?' 'Yes, Doctor, it's all right for me.' Up comes Braund's leg break. I go up the pitch for an off drive and Cranfield didn't play again for a fortnight. By the bye Cranfield was one of the only two bowlers I ever played against who occasionally made the ball swerve *downwards*. The first ball I had from him was a full pitch waist high – I was thinking of hitting it for 6 when suddenly it seemed to *dive*. It finished as a yorker. And I shouldn't have stopped it if I hadn't taken in a much lighter bat by mistake. It was Ollivierre's. Having played that ball – my first – I had to ask 'W.G.' if I might change it. He looked quite puzzled – stroked his beard a couple of times before he gave permission and told me to hurry up. . . .

More modern captains have been known to have superstitions especially about setting aside one particular coin to toss up for choice of innings. Brian Sellers, for instance, always uses the same five shilling piece. Peter Eckersley when tossing for Lancashire tossed with his favourite four shilling piece. Percy Chapman religiously stuck to his lucky half-sovereign. As to 'W.G.' I think if he had used anything but any old penny I should have noticed it. . . .

The Coronation Week matches in 1902, it was at one time thought, might have to be postponed because King Edward VII was suddenly taken seriously ill. But that sporting gentleman insisted that only the Coronation ceremony must be put back and all outdoor fixtures must be carried out. This was great good fortune for Derbyshire because that county was to receive a visit from Dr. W. G. Grace with his London County eleven, which included his son 'W.G.' Junior (who wore glasses and was not a great player although he did get his Blue at the Varsity) and W. L. Murdoch, the genial and former Australian captain. I won the toss and in real King's weather we batted first on a perfect wicket. Everything was in favour of the batsmen and, when it came my turn to go in, the bowlers were pretty tired. I attacked every one of them and reached my century in an hour and a quarter – my score rose quickly to 140 when 'W.G.' proceeded to make another bowling change. But I reminded him of his threat the previous night to put Billy Murdoch on to bowl. 'All right,' rejoined 'W.G.', 'come on, Billy – you have a go.' I was very anxious to get 150 and Billy was no bowler. The first four balls were almost out of reach on the offside, so I didn't bother with them. The fifth – oh hurrah – a long hop a foot outside the off stump. Over went my left leg and I clouted the ball good and hard straight into the hands of 'W.G.' quite close in at point and amid a roar of laughter, out I had to go. 149 – caught W. G. Grace, bowled W. L. Murdoch – amplifying this – I think quite excusably – caught by a great England captain from a ball bowled by a great Australian captain. The next ball – the last of the over – saw Walter Sugg attempt a huge drive – miss it altogether and get stumped. Billy Murdoch put on his sweater but 'W.G.' interposing asked him if he wasn't going to have another over. 'Not bally likely' replied Billy Murdoch – it was a favourite expression of his – 'I've got two for none – I'm top of the bowling averages and I'm going to stay top.' And so he did – the records are there for all to see. Look up your 1903 *Wisden*.

That Coronation year match at Derby found all the luck going my way. An imp of mischief – or of inspiration – call it what you will – prompted me to put myself on bowling. For months past – indeed throughout the previous winter I had been practising bowling an in-swerver – a ball swinging in, very late, from the off. About the third over I tried it on 'W.G.'. For once in a way he was caught napping. It was on his off stump and he played forward to it but the very late swerve came off – beat the bat and struck him on the pad. I made a triumphant appeal and the umpire didn't hesitate in giving the Old Man out. He walked off at once but the tone of his voice when he called out 'Oh, Bertie' made me wonder whether I had done right in being so enthusiastic.

In the second innings I decided to have another bowl and again luck was with me for I managed to send down a late swerver which not only pitched on the blind spot but fairly hurried from the pitch and clean bowled him. So for a spell I mingled with the Gods. In one and the same match W. G. Grace lbw b. Lawton and W. G. Grace b. Lawton. Can you wonder that when moments of deep depression occur – as they sometimes do to all – I rise into my cloud of memories, float about amid recollections of that Coronation match and parachute so softly, so gently back to earth.

Here is something which modern batsmen might well consider. I can only suppose it was the result of some unhappy experience which 'W.G.' had undergone in the past. I suppose most of us – at one time or another – have been caught at the wicket or in the slips off the shoulder of the bat, and we have done nothing about it. As I say it had probably happened to 'W.G.' because he made a point of having the shoulders of his bat rounded off.

He was a kindly soul, 'W.G.', especially with me, but I think I scared him once. It was in a Gentlemen v. Players match at the Oval and an hour before lunch our wicket keeper, M. W. Payne got hurt and went off. I put on the pads until the interval after which Lord Dalmony – now the Earl of Rosebery – took my place as I was more useful in the long field. 'W.G.' went on bowling and sent a ball to Jack Gunn just outside his leg stump. Jack Gunn was inclined to let the ball hit his bat. I flung myself down to try and catch one ball. I touched it but couldn't quite hold it. 'W.G.' called out 'I shouldn't do that, Bertie, you might get killed'. I was overkeen and quite willing to take the risk. A similar thing happened a couple of overs later and again I couldn't quite make the catch. 'W.G.' made no further comment but took himself off at the end of the over. Yes, I really think I scared him.

A word on 'W.G.'s' stance at the wicket. We were all taught in those days to stand with one foot on either side of the crease and let the weight of the body rest mainly on the foot behind the crease. 'W.G.' always did this, but he did more, he was a right hand bat, of course, and while the bowler was taking his run his left heel was on the ground but the toe was in the air. I can only remember Jack Hobbs and ocasionally George Gunn who used similar methods. And 'W.G.' always had his bat well up in the air behind him before the bowler let go of the ball. Ranji and Archie MacLaren also made this a practice.

Another point well worthy of note was that you could always see several inches of bat handle below 'W.G.'s' right hand. Nowadays the advantage of that is all too often overlooked, I think.

I can remember another occasion when a query of mine almost made 'W.G.' blush. I had noticed that in one match, in which his side had more than ample time to win, he had declared the innings closed when his own score was 93 not out. This puzzled me considerably. I thought that either there had been no scoreboard or that he had suddenly been taken ill. So the next time I met him I tackled him on the subject and enquired the reason. Do you know he was quite shy about it but eventually and obviously reluctantly, he said 'Well, I'll tell you, Bertie, until that match I had made every score from 0 to 100 excepting 93!' Dear old 'W.G.'. Just imagine how he had to engineer matters to get exactly 93. Fancy his feeling, had he been 92 – run a short single and have it converted to a five by an overthrow to the boundary – whereupon he would have had to start all over again. Actually I believe he was 89 and made things quite positive and secure by declining to score again until he could make dead certain of a boundary. Various names of cricketers have been put forward as better batsmen than 'W.G.'. I have never heard any claim to have anywhere near reached that record of 'W.G.' – it's worth repeating – 'Every score from 0 to 100'.

It was about this time that I received from some cricketing friends in New York, a cablegram inviting me to take a team to the United States for a month's tour, the team to include W. G. Grace. I saw the Old Man and sounded him on the subject. He just stroked his beard and gently but firmly declined. I couldn't shake him. I cabled back to America to say I could not bring 'W.G.' but that I could get together a really strong side which would include W. L. Murdoch and the one and only G. L. Jessop – but they wouldn't have it – 'W.G.' must go along or the project be dropped. It was dropped. A great pity for a handsome sum had been mentioned for expenses. . . .

But talking about 'W.G.'s' ability to spot winners, let me take you back to 1905 Easter Monday when the opening cricket match was at the Oval between Surrey and London County. I think Surrey batted first. 'W.G.' led us out to the wickets and was watching to see who were coming in to open the Surrey innings. I noticed it was Tom Hayward and a nicely built clean looking lad. I was just alongside 'W.G.' and he turned to me and said, 'Bertie, have a good look at this young fellow coming in with Tom. Unless I'm very much mistaken he's going to be a star'. I did have a good look – he made 38 or 39 in great style before being bowled hitting across a straight one. As he was walking away 'W.G.' called after him, 'You'll have to get rid of that stroke, Jack' and a rueful reply came back, 'Yes, I'm afraid so, Doctor'. Well that young fellow was none other than Jack Hobbs about whom the year before he died, Ranji said to me – 'pick a world eleven – the best of all time and you would probably *have* to put in Jack Hobbs as 12th man'. And with that opinion I can heartily agree.

I remember 'W.G.' once taking a new bat to open the innings. The wicket was very fast and one or two balls were flying about a bit. 'W.G.' only made some thirty odd before being caught in the slips. When he returned to our dressing room and someone remarked on the red stain on the *edge* of that new bat, 'W.G.' was ready for him. He just said 'My boy, what is the good of having an edge on your bat if you don't use it?'

'W.G.' liked to give a pat on the back indirectly as it were. At the Crystal Palace London County had a two-day fixture with Wiltshire. In the late afternoon I was in the long field and the light was very poor – the lovely ground was surrounded by high trees and Wiltshire's Star batsman and a good 'un, J. E. Stevens was knocking 'em about a bit. Then he drove one hard in my direction and I managed to catch it with both hands over my head, near the boundary. As usual I walked in towards the rest of the team but Stevens remained at his crease. Out came 'W.G.'s' question, 'Did you catch it, Bertie?' 'Why yes' I said throwing the ball to him, whereupon 'W.G.' called to Stevens and said 'If he catches 'em like that in the dark you can guess how he does it in the daylight?'

One letter from 'W.G.' would have been my most cherished possession, but alas it has been destroyed. I have however seen a photograph of it in one of E. H. B. Sewell's books. It was written to Sewell by 'W.G.' after Sewell had asked the Old Man how he would counteract the ultra fast and bumping bowling by means of which one visiting Australian eleven were wiping out our Test teams. 'W.G.' wrote 'I would pick A. E. Lawton and send him in to knock them off their length'.

I have been trying so hard to picture the Old Man's suits. I never saw him in navy blue or wearing pin-striped trousers. I think his clothes were always of the same sort of very dark grey – and a modern crease in his trousers would be unthinkable. And I can't remember that he ever wore a bowler or a straw hat. Yet in flannels or in mufti he would always have that indefinable something that stands a man out before his fellows.

I think the last time I played in a first class cricket match with 'W.G.' was at the Oval in 1906. The occasion was the Gentlemen v. Players game and it was particularly eventful because the first day coincided with 'W.G.'s' birthday. Born as he was in 1848 it was his 58th anniversary. Everyone was hugely delighted when the 'Old Man' won the toss and went in first himself. The weather was perfect and the pitch one of Sam Apted's very best. Naturally, 'W.G.' had a marvellous reception from the huge crowd. From the very first over we all saw that he was in his very best form. He was never in any difficulty at all. He just played every ball exactly on its merits. Except that he didn't attempt to hit a six he disclosed every one of the gamut of cricket strokes in his repertoire. His timing and placing of his shots was absolutely masterly and players and spectators alike were entranced. He had set himself one particular target which the crowd was quick to sense. That was to score at least 58 runs – one for each year of his life. When he reached his 50 the applause was terrific and when he cut a ball down to deep third man and just walked along the wicket for his 58th run the crowd went mad. They cheered and cheered for minutes. They said we had watched a model 'knock' which the Press unanimously agreed was the perfect object lesson for old and young. Never once had he lifted the ball off the ground – nor had a single one been edged. Every time he sent it exactly where he wanted to. I have not seen anyone play an innings, before or since, which gave me such sheer joy. 'W.G.' rather naturally, surged after that. He added another 16 or 17 and then got out. Just think it over – a man of his bulk, at the age of 58 with his black beard fast growing grey captaining the Gentlemen's XI against the Professionals in the second biggest match of the year. His side was said to include five of the biggest hitters in the Country and such was the inspiration to us of his marvellous effort that each of us came off either in the first or the second innings. And that seemed to please him every bit as much as his own triumph. He was like that, was 'W.G.'.

In the closing years of his life I saw little of 'W.G.'. In the early part of 1915 I had to make a business trip to Boston U.S.A., and returned from New York on the February trip of the ill-fated *Lusitania*. As soon as I reached home I was told of the passing of 'W.G.' – of how a Zeppelin airship had cruised over his house one cold frosty night – of how he had gone out into his garden and remained for a spell shaking his fist at it muttering 'You devils, you devils'. He caught a chill, pneumonia set in, and very soon there had left this earth the greatest Cricketer this country – nay, this world, has ever seen – Dr. William Gilbert Grace. My Cricket hero! My friend!! My 'W.G.'.

Unpublished, ms. in Lord's Library, 1948

A PATIENT once knocked at the door of W.G.'s house in Bristol: 'Is Dr. Grace in?' The reply came back quickly, 'Of course he's in; he's been batting since lunch-time on Tuesday'.

— 12 —

RADIO REMINISCENCES

Recalling the Great Doctor

P. F. WARNER

THE first time I ever saw W. G. Grace was at Lord's, in May, 1887, at the match between M.C.C. and Sussex. It was a bitterly cold afternoon, and I sat in the seats directly in front of the old tennis court, and saw C. A. Smith, the well-known actor of today, bowling down the wickets. W.G. was out when I arrived, but during the luncheon interval he passed quite close to me, and I gazed with undisguised admiration, not to say awe, on the most dominating personality the cricket world has ever seen. Imagine a man of six feet two inches in height, broad in proportion, with a long black beard, swarthy face, rather small but twinkling eyes, and with an M.C.C. cap crowning his coal black hair. His hands were enormous, as were his feet, which evoked the admiration of an Australian squatter, who remarked that he was worth £3 a week and his 'tucker' just to walk about and crush the cockroaches!

The first occasion on which I actually played cricket with him was in the Gloucestershire and Middlesex match at Clifton in August, 1894.

I recollect vividly his arrival on the College ground. He was wearing white flannel trousers, a black cut-away coat, and a black hat – half top hat, half bowler, and his cheery cry of 'Eight o'clock tonight, Webbie; don't forget; it's down the well'; referred to his invitation that the Middlesex amateurs should dine with him that evening, and that the champagne was on ice.

Wherever he went during the intervals of the match, he was followed by an admiring crowd, and I need hardly say how delighted and proud I was when he spoke to me and said that he hoped I would get some runs.

His brother, E. M. Grace (almost as great a personality as W.G. himself) was playing in this match for Gloucestershire, and I had the distinction of being missed by him at point – an unusual bit of luck, for E.M. lives in history as one of the greatest fieldsmen that the world has ever seen. There was a great deal of chattering when he missed me, and cries from W.G. of 'You ought to have caught it, Ted. You know you ought to have caught it.' Jack Board, the wicketkeeper, also joined in the conversation, and I marvelled to myself that so much importance should be attached to the missing of a colt who was playing in only his second match for Middlesex.

E.M. was Coroner for one of the Gloucestershire Divisions, and the story goes that in another Middlesex and Gloucestershire match the batsman was cut over and fell to the ground. E.M., who was batting at the other end, walked up the wicket, and as the fielding side crowded round the injured batsman, a man in the crowd shouted out 'Why don't you hold an inquest on him, Coroner?' whereupon E.M. said to Mr. A. J. Webbe (the Middlesex captain), 'Excuse me, Webbie, I can't stand that,' and off he darted, brandishing his bat, to that portion of the ground from which the remark had come. The offender, seeing E.M. in full cry towards him, made post-haste out of the ground, and E.M. returned to apologize, and repeat, 'I can't stand that, I won't stand that.'

But to return to W.G. He first played for the Gentlemen against the Players in the year 1864, when he was only sixteen years old, and in the course of his career he took part in no fewer than eighty-five Gentlemen and Players matches.

He was, of course, always first choice for England, and he played both for the Gentlemen, at Lord's, and for England against Australia when he was over fifty years of age. His last Test match was at Nottingham in 1899. After that game he retired, saying he thought it was time to make room for a younger man.

He made the first 100 in a Test match in England, between England and Australia, in the first Test match ever played in this country, at Kennington Oval, in September, 1880.

There is a good story told about him in the England v. Australia match, at Lord's, in June, 1896. Australia had been dismissed for 53 by Lohmann and Richardson, the great Surrey bowlers, on a splendid wicket, and W.G. and Stoddart came out to open England's first innings. Jones, a man of superb build and physique, and a very fast bowler, opened the bowling from the Pavilion end to W. G. Grace. The first ball was very fast and very short, got up quickly, and went through W.G.'s beard. The wicketkeeper, standing back, lost sight of the ball in W.G.'s beard, and the ball bumped up against the screen with a tremendous thud, 4 byes being scored. W.G. walked up the wicket and, in his well-known voice, said: 'Where the devil are you bowling to, Jonah?' to which Jones made a good reply: 'Sorry, Doctor, she slipped!' I do not know whether the idea was to intimidate 'The Old Man' (as W.G. was affectionately called), but it had no effect on him, for he made 68 of the best before being caught at slip off George Giffen, the W.G. of Australia, who died recently.

It is one of my proudest memories that I had the distinction of going in first with W.G. on more than one occasion – in Gentlemen v. Players at the Oval, North v. South at Lord's, and in M.C.C. matches against the Australians and others.

I can assure you we were a queer pair as we left the Pavilion – he 18 stone, with his black beard and flaming M.C.C. cap. I little more than half his weight, certainly half his width, about three inches shorter, and in a cap – looking, perhaps, many years younger than I really was.

There was nothing W.G. didn't know about the game. He inspired confidence in his team, and, if something of a martinet, had a heart of gold and a most kindly disposition.

At the same time strict discipline existed in any team of which he was captain, and woe betide the man who was in any degree slack in the field or who he thought was slack. I remember him dropping heavily on Wrathall, one of the Gloucestershire professionals, and a member of the M.C.C. ground staff, in a match between M.C.C. and Australians at Lord's in 1899.

Now Wrathall was an exceptionally keen and hard-working cricketer, a particularly good outfield; but for some reason W.G. thought that a little punishment drill would do him good. So he made him field at long-on to J. T. Hearne's bowling at the Pavilion end, and at long off to C. L. Townsend, who was at the end opposite the Pavilion. This entailed a walk, or rather, a run of something like 150 yards between the overs, and I ventured to say to W.G., 'Let me go out in the country to Townsend, as Wrathall has a long journey between the overs,' and he replied, 'No, no, Harry is lazy; it will do him good.' It was in this match that he took six wickets for twenty-nine runs. The Australians had something like two hundred and sixty runs on the board with only four men out, but after pulling at his beard – a habit of his when he was worried, W.G. said in his rather high-pitched voice, 'Here, give me the ball,' and almost at once the Australian wickets began to fall in rapid succession.

He used, too, to keep Fred Roberts, the old Gloucestershire fast left hander, a pleasant and amusing character, up to the mark, and the following conversation would often be heard: 'Keep your arm up, Fred, keep it up'; and it is alleged, though I do not vouch for its accuracy, that, standing at point, he once said to Roberts, who had just hit the batsman on the pads: 'Why don't you appeal, Fred?' and Roberts replied, 'I was waiting for you, sir!'

He was keen to get a batsman out, and on occasions his zeal possibly got the better of him, but his was a lovable character, and he was always very nice and encouraging to young cricketers, and in his old age he was very welcome in any dressing room, for he never 'crabbed' anybody, and had always an excuse for the batsmen who had failed.

He expected bowlers to work very hard, and it is on record that he once kept S. M. J. Woods, the great fast bowler with a beautiful slow ball, on bowling in a Gentlemen v. Players at the Oval from 11.30 to 5.30 without a rest! He was so strong himself that he did not always realize the limitations of the human frame.

He was extraordinarily popular, and two instances of the affection in which he was held may be given here. The first occasion was at a dinner given to A. E. Stoddart in London, after his successful tour in Australia in 1894–5. W.G. was always very fond of Stoddart, and promised that nothing would prevent him from coming to the dinner. At the time Gloucestershire was playing Somerset at Bristol, the famous match in which W.G. made 288 and completed his hundred centuries, a feat which was celebrated by champagne being brought on to the pitch. The game lasted late into the third day, and W.G. could not get to the dinner until about a quarter to nine. As he walked into the room everyone stood up and cheered him for at least two minutes. The old man beamed all over his face and was obviously much touched.

The second occasion was when, on his fiftieth birthday, July 18, 1898, he led the Gentlemen into the field at Lord's in the great annual match between Amateurs and Professionals. As he came down the pavilion steps the pavilion and ground rose at him and gave him a reception such as even he, accustomed as he was to the applause of the multitude, must have appreciated beyond measure.

In his prime wickets were not nearly so good as they are now, but W.G. himself told me that the Oval, Fenner's, Brighton, Canterbury, and the Clifton College ground were perfect for run getting. He was the finest possible player of fast bowling, and literally 'killed' the fast bowlers of the late 'sixties, 'seventies, and early 'eighties.

I remember once asking him whether there was any bowler or any type of bowling which he did not quite fancy, and his reply was: 'I don't mind how or what they bowled if I was in form, but the faster they bowled the better I liked them.' He is said to have remarked that he was glad he didn't have to play the googly, but it is quite certain that he would have mastered that as he did every other type of bowling, had he been called upon to face it.

When I knew him he must have weighed nearly 18 stone, and this naturally made it rather difficult for him to 'get at' a slow bowler, but I should imagine that in his youth what he said was perfectly true, that it didn't matter who bowled to him if he was in form.

He was not what would be called a pretty batsmen. He lacked, for instance, the grace of style of a Woolley or a Hobbs or a Palairet, and he represented sheer force and power rather than style. He was a beautiful late cutter even in his old age, and was exceedingly strong on the on-side, where he placed the ball with great accuracy. He was a very fine on-driver and his defence was extremely good.

It is difficult to compare the cricketers of one generation with those of another. There will be found people who will say that W.G. was better than any other batsman who has ever lived, whilst others will declare that W.G. was not so good as Hobbs or Macartney or Ranji or Trumper. I venture to think, however, that if one maintains a right sense of proportion, a sound opinion would be that a great cricketer in one generation would always be a great cricketer in another.

Conditions at cricket change, and no doubt will continue to change, just as they do in warfare, but I take it that Julius Caesar, or Hannibal, or Napoleon – not one of whom knew anything of machine guns, heavy artillery, magazine rifles, and gas attacks – would be great generals in the field if they were alive today; just as Nelson, who never dreamt of battle cruisers steaming 30 knots an hour, 16-in. guns, mines, submarines, and torpedoes with a run of 15,000 yards, would be a great admiral in a modern naval action.

It may, I think, be said with certainty that W.G. created modern cricket, that he popularized it, and that he caused thousands to flock to see the game where before there had been but hundreds. So long as cricket is played Grace's name will occupy the first place. He was the champion. No one before or since has ever been styled that, and it is doubtful whether anyone ever will be. He was unique in English cricket, a great figure in the nation's life, and was as well known by sight as even Mr. Lloyd George or Mr. Winston Churchill.

After his death the Marylebone Committee decided to erect a Memorial Gate at Lord's, and members of the Committee were asked to send in their ideas of a suitable epitaph to be placed on the gates which now stand at the members' entrance. Scores of suggestions were received, some, I am told, in Latin, but none quite satisfied the Committee until Colonel F. S. Jackson (now Sir Stanley Jackson, the Governor of Bengal), a very great cricketer himself, sent in his idea. It was quite short, quite simple, and the words are to be read on the gates at Lord's today: 'W. G. Grace, the great cricketer, 1848–1915'.

Great bowlers, great batsmen, great fielders, or a combination of all three, may arise in the future, but W.G. will ever remain THE Great Cricketer.

Savoy Hill, 1928

I Knew a Man

A. C. MACLAREN

MY first introduction to W. G. Grace took place in the Old Trafford pavilion, and I well remember watching the great man tying his M.C.C. sash round his waist, as I gazed in admiration at what appeared to me to be a very genial Father Christmas with a black beard. He was of massive proportions, and was more suited to the role of Father Christmas than of a great cricketer. The whole place was alive with merriment, as was always the case when W.G. was present. He put out an enormous paw, saying, 'Ow are you, little man?', and then continued his chaff surrounded by Lancashire members and one or two players.

So inspired was I by this great man's presence, that when my father said, 'Now, my boy, you have seen the Captain of England', I informed my mother that same day that I also would be Captain of England when I grew up. It was an extraordinary coincidence that he should have wired to me at the end of his Test cricket career to take his place as Captain.

I had played under W.G. on the previous visit of the Australians, and my affection for this dear old man was such that it inspired my own cricket ability. For I could not have wished to serve under a more encouraging, sympathetic, and appreciative Captain. There was always the feeling on my part of complete security whenever I had the good fortune to be one of his team. The delight expressed by him on every occasion, at anything out of the ordinary on the part of the fieldsman, acted as an incentive to every man to produce his best. Indeed, I will go further – the winning atmosphere his presence created seemed to make everyone produce *more* than his best.

For some reason a certain few held the opinion that W.G. was not as good a Captain as would be expected. This was not my view. In all the matched I played with or against him I can think of no occasion on which adverse criticism would have been justified. He invited most generously valued opinion. I ought to make it clear to my listeners that I was too young ever to have seen the champion at the zenith of his career – in those years when one *can* only be at one's best – for he was distinctly an old man for a Test cricketer when I first played under him.

This, however, did not prevent him from being top scorer in one of the three Test matches in which I played under his captaincy, and again in the Gentlemen *v*. Players match at Lord's on his fiftieth birthday against the cream of English bowling, on a difficult wicket – a really wonderful performance.

We all know that as a batsman his methods were of the soundest: he had every stroke on the board at his command, while his concentration was most marked. An outstanding feature was the accuracy with which he placed the ball between the fieldsmen, particularly in the cutting strokes through the slips. One can truthfully say that on all wickets and against every type of bowling he remained supreme. I once asked him which bowler he liked least of all. He paused for a moment, then rapped out: 'Archie, I love 'em all'.

People have asked if W.G. ever appeared to be nervous, and on my referring this question to him he replied: 'Well, I always feel better after my luncheon'. Certainly his play gave no indication that he was ever nervous. He demonstrated to all of us that wet wickets and hard wickets all came alike to him.

Which reminds me of an amusing incident that took place before my playing days, when Yorkshire were playing Gloucestershire. W.G., whilst batting, was handed a telegram which in those days was always brought out to the player on the field. Tom Emmett, the left-hand bowler – a rare Yorkshire character – appeared to be interested. W.G. called out to him: 'I've got my diploma, Tom'. Shortly after W.G. slipped and sat on the muddy wicket to hear Tom call out as he picked himself up: 'Ah see thou'st got diploma all right, Doctor'.

W.G. was always held up as a true model of physical fitness, and my mother was the first to tell me that he neither drank nor smoked; but it was not long before I had good reason to doubt the accuracy of my mother's statement, for I now frequently had the opportunity of seeing for myself. Certainly he was most careful of his diet, but on one occasion after a long innings, when, as often, he was the guest of the evening, one of his team, noticing he had gone beyond two glasses of champagne, remarked to him: 'I thought you said, W.G., you never had more than two glasses of wine at dinner?' 'Ted', replied W.G., 'I said I could drink any *given* quantity.'

The very soundness of his successes left no room for any lack of confidence in himself at any time, even when age was overtaking him. This is showed in his reply to my expression of sorrow at an unusually early return to the pavilion after opening the innings against Australia; 'There's a second innings yet, Archie'. Another saying never to be forgotten by cricketers, and which should still give all food for thought, came from him. 'The beauty of this game lies in the knowledge that there is always something to be learnt, every day you play it.' And this from the champion of champions.

I can't remember ever seeing W.G. hit by the ball, let alone hurt, and I might also add that he never missed a match through ill-health. A. N. Hornby, my first Captain, a great one and a fine international player, told me of an occasion when, owing to lack of accommodation, he shared a bedroom with W.G. As he opened the door in the morning W.G. woke up and said: 'Where are you off to, Monkey?' 'I am just going to have my cold bath.' 'Oo', said W.G, ''Ow you do make me shudder.'

His dominating personality on the cricket field is well illustrated by an incident which I witnessed in a match between Lancashire and Gloucestershire. He was particularly quick to notice if any of the opponents thought the umpire was generously giving him the benefit of the doubt in an l.b.w. decision. In this match I was fielding first slip, and an appeal from Mold, who had hit the old man on the leg, was disallowed. I asked Mold quietly at the end of the over his opinion of the umpire's decision – to receive an irritable reply: 'It would have sent the middle peg flying'. W.G. happened to overhear this remark and he called out: 'What's that you say – what's that you say, why you have been *throwing* at me this last half-hour.' But afterwards in his calmer moments he apologized to Mold for what he had said.

Only once did W.G. put the boxing gloves on with me. On a soft wicket, after hooking the slow bowler Charlie Townsend to the outfield, stationed at mid-wicket, I slipped and knocked my leg stump almost flat with my left foot in starting to run at the completion of my stroke. W.G. immediately shouted "E's out, 'e's out, toss 'er up! toss 'er up! 'E's out, 'e's out!' So as I was in the middle of my run I joined in the chorus, calling out to the umpire 'I'm not out, I'm not out'. Nice behaviour on the part of two international bats! When I got to the other end W.G., instead of appealing to the umpire, walked towards me with lowered head, like an infuriated bull, and said: 'Ain't you going out, Archie?' 'Not until the umpire gives me out', I replied slowly and emphatically. Then he turned to the umpire and said: 'Well, 'ow was it?' 'Not out', said the umpire. Then the band began to play with a vengeance, and, as I made 70 more runs after this happening, W.G. had a howl for every run made, which I received in silence . . .

When I am asked who was the best in any department of the game I start my reply with the words 'always excepting W.G. . . .' A world-famous international in his prime told me he doubted whether W.G. was quite the player he was ever made out to be. I replied: 'Wait till you are fifty, when you won't look so pretty at the wicket, and then get top score in the biggest match of the year on a bowler's wicket'.

We who never saw W.G. in his prime can only guess how great he must have been in his younger days. Where he excelled in his old age for a cricketer was in his knowledge of the limitations imposed upon him only by increasing years. He never attempted to do with the bat what his age prohibited, but rightly preferred to *wait* for his now fewer opportunities for scoring in front of the wicket than to *make* them as he used to do in his earlier days. He retained in a marvellous manner almost to the last those occasional taps through the slips off the shorter pitched ball outside the off stump, always most cleverly placed to beat the fieldsman; as well as dealing in the telling manner, which was probably one of the strongest features of his batting in his palmy days, with any ball on his legs.

He was rarely, if ever, at fault in throwing a 'cross' bat at the ball of driving length on the off-side. He would send it humming to the on-side boundary over short mid-on's head – rather than play the more orthodox stroke, through the covers. In the December of his cricketing life, when he used to captain London County, it was not too easy to get as many of the counties to play against him as he wished, owing to their already well-filled programme.

On one occasion, however, Lancashire, during my captaincy, came to the rescue, gladly giving up their three days' holiday in the middle of the season to give him a game. So along came W.G. and his merry men, among them W. L. Murdoch, the famous Australian Captain and batsman and a former opponent of W.G. It was out of the question not to put our full strength against any side of the head of which was the old man himself, to say nothing of Billy Murdoch, who in Australia was held in the same reverence as our own champion in this country. I have the most vivid recollections of this game.

The old man won the toss from me on a perfect wicket, and out stepped these two stalwarts to provide a batting treat, which at that period of their lives was beyond all expectations.

They both topped the century. It was remarkable that the effectiveness of their cutting allowed no weakening of the slip positions, thereby making their driving more telling when the bowler required that extra field on the off, who could not be spared. Here was a spectacle provided by two past masters of batting, whose repertoire of strokes was little less than it had been in their hey-day.

The conditions were perfectly suited to these two old men. Sunshine in a cloudless sky, warmth in the air and a perfect pitch beneath them.

What more could they want? I am sure that no two cricketers ever enjoyed themselves more, or could have been more completely satisfied with their exhibition of batting – ever to remain a delight to those who had the fortune to witness it.

As I am speaking now, I can see W.G. and Billy Murdoch standing at the top of the steps of the pavilion as they were leaving the ground at 4 o'clock on the last day, just as we were dismissing the end batsmen – waving and calling to us 'Good-bye, Archie' – 'Good-bye, Billy', 'Good-bye, W.G.'

THE LISTENER, *October, 1935*

In the Gallery of the Great Victorians

DUDLEY CAREW

THE year 1948, being itself, as it were, a centenary year and having a great deal on its hands, may well consider that it needn't bother about so small a thing as the anniversary date of a man who merely happened to be supremely good at a game. And if that was all, it would doubtless be right. It is far from being all, however, for W. G. Grace, was not only the greatest cricketer who has ever lived, but a character who can take his burly, bearded place in the Gallery of the great Victorians. He is as imperturbably proof in death against the pin-pricks of the lesser pupils of the Lytton Strachey school as he was in life against the worst that fast bowlers and inferior wickets could do. But, again, he was more than that, more than a batsman who would send the hansoms jingling up the St. John's Wood Road when the news reached the clubs that he was not out at Lord's. Let's look once more at the centenary the year itself is celebrating.

1848, the year of revolutions, of the Communist Manifesto, when the towering shadow of Metternick ceased to dominate the European scene and Louis Phillipe found himself turned out of France, was in England only another year in the long procession which saw the proletariat struggling free of the worst horrors of the Industrial Revolution. The people were beginning to find that they actually had time to do something except sleep, eat and work. Not very much time, extremely little in fact, but it was there, that precious lapse in the iron rhythm beaten out by the necessitous hours, and leisure found room to breathe. The people were making their demands felt; political demands in

Europe; in England, demands for the entertainments and excitements which would make the new conceptions of leisure and holidays worth while. In the country men are able to fashion and take part in their own sports, but the great urban population which had come into being towards the end of the nineteenth century was at a loss when it came to the question of amusing itself. The days of the cock-pit were over; those of the packed football stadiums, the dog-tracks, and the pools as yet undreamed of, but in the manner in which W.G. played on the lawn of a country house in Gloucestershire, the future was shaping itself.

Cricket, of course, did not begin with W.G. – its history is far longer than the younger generation is inclined to believe, long enough for the confusion between Julius Caesar, the Roman Emperor, and Julius Caesar, the Surrey batsman, to be excusable. The glories of little Hambledon were already a legend when W.G. was born, but the game was capricious in its appeal and had only lately ceased to be a preserve of the aristocracy – an affair of wagers as well as of wickets. County cricket, as it is understood to-day, was unknown, although Kent and Surrey had had their champions and their triumphs. But, when W.G. was making his presence felt among the clubs of the West Country, the chief attraction of the season was afforded by such touring teams as the United XI and the All England XI, which journeyed up and down the country playing against odds and drawing crowds. It was all haphazard, however, and W.G. was destined first to turn the technique of the game from a one-stringed instrument into a many-chorded lyre, and then (a natural sequel and even more important), to transform cricket, and indirectly other sports, from being casual amusements into organized businesses tied up with, and more or less dependent on, finance. Cricket has never been the most popular sport with the masses, although it comes a good second, but it pointed the way for the formation of football leagues. Those clubs of the North and Midlands with their dark and splendid names, Preston North End, West Bromwich Albion, Aston Villa, and Blackburn Rovers, which now draw crowds of 60,000 people or so and buy and sell their players, must have gained some encouragement to start from the fact that cricket under W.G. had proved that there was a public eager to pay for the privilege of watching professionals at their own games.

W.G., in other words, was the first 'star', the first box-office draw. There had been great men before him – wasn't W.G. presented with Alfred Mynn's pads by an enthusiast who declared that he alone was worthy to wear them? – but Mynn and Beldham, to say nothing of Lord Frederick Beauclerk and George Osbaldeston, belonged to an age when cricket was more of a private enjoyment than a public spectacle. W.G. was one of the examples of the hour and the man working in perfect collaboration to bring about a state of affairs which was, in any event, inevitable. W.G. hastened the process, hastened it and gave to what might be called 'mass-appeal cricket' the imprint and authority of personality.

'Star', 'box-office' – these terms suggest the conscious showman, the man who knows he has something to sell and is flamboyant in his methods of selling it. But however much W.G., in his later days, may have enjoyed the peculiar and privileged position he occupied on the cricket field and the wider arena of national life, he founded his fame on the sheer mastery of his skill with a cricket bat and a cricket ball. He appears in the mind as a figure something larger and more intimidating than life, bushy and black of beard and brow, a thought shambling in his walk, his M.C.C. cap an oriflame on his head, his bat a toy in broad and cunning hands, but then W.G. is fixed in the public imagination as a man middle-aged in years and a veteran in the game-playing sense of the term . . .

Far otherwise, however, was the boy who . . . turned cricket upside down, made it a science, and established it as a business. When he first played in first-class cricket in 1864, a batsman who scored a couple of centuries and averaged thirty in a season was doing exceptionally well; the ball was generally dominant over a bat which was limited in its conception of stroke-play. W.G.'s elder brother, the redoubtable 'Coroner', had already shown what could be done with a stout heart, a keen eye, a contempt for orthodoxy, and a cross-bat, but W.G. tamed the fast bowling of his time by surer and more effective methods. Before him, batsmen were inclined to be either 'forward' or 'back' players – they were born like it, as they were born little Liberals or little Conservatives – but, and here is the point of Ranji's one-stringed into many-chorded analogy, W.G. combined in his masterful and capacious self the best elements of both styles. The ball that demanded back play was played back to. The next was met with the left foot and bat coming forward, and informing a style that set itself determinedly to eliminate all possible error was an immense physical strength and a personality to match it.

Taming is a tame word to apply to W.G.'s treatment of the fast bowling that was fashionable in his early days; he did not so much tame as annihilate it, sweep it out of his path, scatter it like chaff. He broke the bowler's hearts and so bemused their heads that they did not know where to pitch the ball. While W.G. revelled throughout his career in bowlers who tried to make the ball whistle through his beard, he was almost as great a master against the turning ball on the sticky pitch, although here, perhaps, Shrewsbury was his equal. 'Give me Arthur,' said the old man, towards the end of his life, when asked who was the greatest batsman he had ever played with, and he must have seen in his mind's eye Arthur Shrewsbury, sure and utterly concentrated, watching the viciously turning ball right on to the bat.

Those who delight in holding up the vast aggregate and averages made by modern batsmen in general, and Bradman in particular, against the modest totals of W.G. and argue further that W.G. had not the googly problem to solve, forget the simplest of all facts, the fact that every man's performance is prescribed by the circumstances of his time. W.G. could not play the googly, because there was no googly to play, but to maintain that the ball Bosanquet invented would have beaten a man who thought and lived cricket, who bestrode the field like a Colossus, who dominated cricket, who was a legend in his own lifetime and had overcome in himself all that the bowlers, pitches, climes and circumstances could do against him, is to argue in the teeth of all sense and probability. It's possible W.G. would not have liked the googly although ordinary county batsmen have learned to play it – Bradman himself has caricatured his own style against certain forms of attack – but he would certainly have taken it in his majestic stride.

There are reference books enough to tell of the number of runs and centuries W.G. made, the number of wickets he took with that slow, easy-tossed bowling, which was not as simple as it looked, the number of catches he snatched . . . getting down to the ball with surprising agility for a man of his bulk. There he is, the champion of champions, turning the tables for the Gentlemen on the Players, leading Gloucestershire, captaining England, the first and commanding link that leads from the careless, tented field to the concrete stadium arena where thousands of pounds tinkle in at the box-office and a nation hangs on the broadcast relay of an innings as intently as on the word of victory or defeat in war . . . Let us clear away the tangle of statistics, the stories of triumph, and peer more closely at the portrait of this man who, in feature and personality, is so characteristic of the age that nurtured him. Mr. Desmond MacCarthy has written recently of the manner in which people who knew Henry James well differ as to the colour of his eyes, and there seems some confusion as to the quality of W.G.'s voice. A mighty parade-ground voice would seem the obvious partner to bulk and beard, but the evidence is clear that actually W.G.'s voice was high-pitched almost to the point of a falsetto squeak and that the accent was distinctive and far from standard English. There is, then, a contradiction between voice and physique, but otherwise the man is splendidly of a piece . . .

The poetry of Matthew Arnold is alone evidence enough that the Victorians were not so complacent as their complacent parodists assume, but for every one who hesitated and faltered, there were half-a-dozen others who drew an inward strength and certainty from the undeniable fact of England's greatness. She *was* great and did not question or analyse her greatness, and they, with ample bodies well stocked with food, and minds furnished with rich, upholstered prejudice, did not question or analyse either. W.G. was not, in the contemporary meaning of the word, a clever man, and whether he wrote his own book on cricket and his early experiences or had it written for him, the result is sadly commonplace. There are few touches of humour or imagination in it, but it would be rash indeed to argue from so frail a premise that the man himself was without those qualities. The modern Englishman, however much he may feel inadequate in the face of the modern world, will defend to the death his possession of a sense of humour. Deny him faith, honour, charity, humanity, and he will allow there is something in what you say, but deny him his sense of humour, and no tigress could be more fierce or passionate in defence of her young. By humour we mean to-day a verbal defensive irony, a smiling disinclination to be impressed, by the worst, or the best that life and the universe can do, but the word did not mean that to the Victorians or to the age immediately preceding it. To them it meant gusto, an excess of high spirits, an overflow of zest. There was no end to the Victorian capacity for the full-hearted employment of their powers to whatever lay to their hand, and the surplus worked itself off in ways which we might find embarrassing. There's nothing, if it is looked at in the right way, in the least astonishing or contradictory in the idea of Mr. and Mrs. Gladstone dancing round their drawing-room singing songs about raggamuffin husbands, and ranty-polin' wives. It is entirely in character, and that zest, that humour, that simplicity, expressed itself in character and seldom found its way into print. When it did, it was transformed, turning up in the disguise of nonsense verse and stories for children, in puns and a general and delibrate inclination towards the more artificial lunacies.

W.G., like others of his time, was content to carry about in his own capacious self his humour, his kindness, and his imagination, to express them in what he was and what he did. His size inevitably suggests comparison with Falstaff and thin indeed would be any estimate of the man which left out that rich sense of enjoyment of the good things of life he shared with the Elizabethan. It was only at the end of his life, however, that Falstaff babbled o' green fields; W.G. spent his days on them. Nevertheless, the two would have got on well enough had they met. They had in common the unconscious ability of making themselves indispensable to any company in which they happened to be in. There is evidence enough in *Henry IV* of the power of attraction Falstaff exercised over his particular circle, and W.G., who had all England for his, could in the same way turn his very presence into a benison and tonic. There must have been an intolerable flatness in the atmosphere of the Boar's Head when Falstaff was not there with his pot of sack before him, and a cricket field empty of W.G. was a cricket field drained of the magic less of technical skill than of sheer personality. W.G. had a way with other things than a bat; he had a way with life. What he knew he knew thoroughly, what he did, he did superbly, and what he was, he was uniquely.

The word 'gamesmanship' is a popular one to-day, and Mr. Stephen Potter, with an impish malice, has set the famous beard on the cover of his treatise on the 'art of winning games without actually cheating'. Even those most earnest in their desire to defend W.G. from the criticism cannot pretend that they do not see the point; but the real point is something, and somewhere, else. Although W.G. wore the M.C.C. cap and Lord's was his home by adoption and right of conquest, he remained to the end of his days a countryman; and he had all of the countryman's sly relish in stealing a march on furriners. Had his circumstances been otherwise, he'd have been a shrewd haggler, a hard driver of bargains – something out of Thomas Hardy – trading up to the limit on his own local knowledge and the ignorance of his prospective client. As it was, he knew the laws and the game of cricket as no-one else and was prepared to take advantage of the fact. He would do everything in his power to win the game. If his opponents were less single-minded, that was their fault and he could not be blamed if he exploited their weakness.

In all those lists enthusiasts draw up on the back of envelopes and menus of an eleven to challenge Mars, all cricketers, living or dead, being miraculously at the top of their form at one and the same time, the name W. G. Grace goes down at once, the first and automatic choice. And in an eleven of Great Victorians, men who stamped their virile personalities on a virile age and moulded the form of the future, W.G. would surely find a place, and an honoured one, going in after Browning, perhaps, with Herbert Spencer to follow him . . .

Broadcasting House, 1948

— 13 —

A FIGURE IN FICTION

Coupled with the Name of 'W.G.'

E. B. V. CHRISTIAN

IT WAS the end of the summer in which the champion reached his hundredth century, and the toast was received uproariously. When the applause subsided the rain had not, and the Chairman looked round for a local orator. His eye fell – it could hardly fail – on The Stout Party. Now a stout man is always exposed to chaff, and he jumped at the opportunity of uttering a long-meditated apology. His few impromptu remarks, he said, would be upon the subject of 'The Stout Cricketer'.

'Mr. Chairman and Gentlemen,' he said, 'far be it from me to say that Dr. Grace is stout; but his form is, let us say, manly. You will remember that the Queen of the Fairies in *Iolanthe*, a lady of noble proportions, remarked that she saw no objection to stoutness in moderation; yet, in men at least, stoutness (like the American judge) is always an object of contempt. In an athlete especially, obesity provokes derision. During the late football season a very competent goalkeeper was unkindly desired by the crowd, merely on account of his waist dimension, to go home and play with his grandchildren. In some sports Falstaff's failing would be a fatal objection; a corpulent coxswain is an impossibility. It says much for the gentle art of cricket that stoutness, if a disadvantage, is not an absolute disqualification. Indeed, one poet of the game, ''W. Bolland'', appeals directly to the fat man's good qualities.

> ''The ball the *stout* cricketer urges
> Cleaves a pathway of peace o'er the plain,''

says the well-known Zingari song. There was something good-natured in the deliveries of Alfred Shaw. The balls which Richardson and Mr. Spofforth urge are not at all peaceful; they lack the geniality of Shaw's style, or Burton's. Doubtless obesity is some incumbrance to a batsman: like honest Jack Falstaff, the stout cricketer feels he is not a swallow, an arrow or a bullet. But he often atones for lack of pace by superior judgment. It is beautiful to see him, standing midway between the wickets, watch the ball going between the fieldsmen to the boundary, "conscious" as the Oxford poet says, "of an unquestioned four."

'Another poet, not named in Dr. Traill's Directory of the Lower Slopes, has celebrated with fine discrimination the joys and sorrows of the stout cricketer. I happened to take up the other day a book called, *Cassandra and Other Poems*, by R. Wheeldon Baddeley, and I read:

> "Not of that sort is he
>   Which lounges by the tent to kill
> The time with levity;
>   Nor loudly boastful of his skill,
> Telling how (in a match you didn't see)
>   He drove a slow for six, or smote to leg
>   A four, or cut a three,
>   Or over a tent-peg
> Tumbled, but made his catch:– not boastful thus
> Is the *stout cricketer* or frivolous."

'These vanities belong to the young men in violent coloured blazers, which used to offend the eye of "F.G." A more tolerant spirit, too, pervades his criticisms of his juniors, although he feels the inferiority of modern cricket to that of his youth,

>   . . . "While
>   Heavily on a bench he sits
> Smoking a pipe, and with a critic's gaze
>   Upon the younger batsmen of his side,
> Recalls old cricket memories from the haze
>   Of time, not loudly to deride,
> But calmly to disparage the wild play
> 'Which, sir, the youngsters of the present day—"

'The stout cricketer's own performances may not rival those of the cracks fresh from college, but are at least respectable. He bats fairly, and, says Mr. Baddeley, "he bowls – swift underhand". So, doubtless, did "Lumpy", the Surrey hero, who helped to beat Kent – Lumpy, whose real name was Stevens, but was called Lumpy "because he was so fat". Of the stout man's fielding the poet says little, save that he struggles to "get peel'd, when he, alack! must after dinner field". That, of course, *is* a trial.

> Sometimes on tented plain,
>   The only veteran there,
> I have seen him, running, mirthful plaudits gain
>   From athlete youth, or girl-spectators fair;
> And I have pitied him as seeming strange,
>   Misplaced among the rest, to him mere boys,
> And fear'd his memories might sadly range
>   Back to fled youth and unreturning joys;
> But these fine fancies don't, I think, occur
> To my respectable *stout cricketer*."

'Perhaps Mr. Baddeley underestimates the sensibility of the stout, as he undervalues their performances. It is not the least of Dr. Grace's services to cricket that he has shown that the race is not always to the slim; that to be pre-eminent in the sport one need be, like the young Falstaff, but an eagle's talon in the waist. And herein he only follows an old tradition of the game. Half the heroes of Hambledon were portly men. Their chief himself, the elder Nyren, was "a very stout man", and Frame, and Aylward. Mr. Ward grew somewhat circular. Lillywhite was "active though thick". Alfred Mynn, that doughty hero, inhabited a form which the poet thought "nobly moulded," but the artists depicted as more than a little redundant. He was, says Mr. Daft, "for a cricketer, the biggest man I ever saw". And Mr. Aislabie (Peter Steele's uncle), immortalized in *Tom Brown*, was "at least 17 stone". The stout cricketer can boast distinguished exemplars. I ask you then to drink with me to the health of "All Stout Cricketers, coupled with the name of W.G."

HOW'S THAT?, *Arrowsmith, 1896*

The Greatest Cricketer That Ever Was

ADAM MANN

HE said that if I wanted to publish this story, I'd got to wait ten years. He'd be gone then. I've kept my part of the bargain; the ten years are up. He has kept his; he died in 1941. I went down to Hastings last year, watched the sparkling Festival cricket, and then walked round to the old sports-shop behind Marine Parade to see if my friend of 1938 was still selling bat-oil, plimsolls, chest-expanders and dart-boards. The shop was still there and plimsolls are on coupons now. But the old man had gone.

I don't suppose, when he made that ten-year stipulation, he realized that 1948 would be the centenary of W.G.'s birth. But that's the ironic way of it. In the summer of this year, when would-be iconoclasts are pointing to Bradman and statistics, when irreverent people are writing to *The Times* to recall that W.G. hated leg-breaks and would have written to the same paper at the first whiff of a googly – in the summer of 1948, just ten years after I heard it in Hastings, I am telling you this story. . . .

The shadows were falling on Nottingham on the evening of June 3rd, 1899. Anyone from the little crowd trickling away over Trent Bridge who had paused in front of the Pavilion would have heard a row blowing up fit to shake Old Parr's tree from its roots. It began when Joe Darling, 'Farmer Joe', stroking his walrus moustache, suggested to W.G. that it was high time someone introduced handicaps into cricket.

'Take this first Test,' he drawled. 'You'd three wickets to go down and you were 134 behind. If we'd finished we must have won by 100, easy. Right, we give you 100 start in the second game. That'll give you a chance, and keep public interest alive.'

For a moment there was stunned silence. In the flickering gaslight little Clem Hill giggled as he watched W.G.'s apple-cheeks purple into monster mulberries. The sheer impiety of Darling's suggestion robbed the English team of speech. Even C. B. Fry was struck dumb.

At last there came a sound which reminded Ranji of the squeal of his favourite shikar elephant at the sight of a man-eater breaking cover. It was W.G. replying for the opposition. He began ridiculing the Australian bowling. 'How anybody ever gets out to such stuff, I don't know.'

'Howell,' murmured Joe Darling; 'yes, he bowled you all over your wicket for one. It was a nice innings, but it came to an end at last.'

The Champion adroitly switched his line of attack. 'But think of the batting strength we had in hand! Only 135 to win! With Ranji set, and Hirst, Hearne and Rhodes to come. Let me tell you, one day young Wilfred will make his Test-match century.'

This was too much for the whole Australian team. Not even Dan Leno at the Alhambra had appealed to their innocent sense of fun as this remark appealed. It was the suave diplomacy of Ranjitsinhji which saved what might have developed into an ugly situation.

'In Nawanagar we have a proverb: "Who can tell what would come if the British were to leave India, or the drawn game were to be played to a finish?"'

'Well, we could play each other again. . . .'

'Excellent! In Nawanagar we have another proverb: "If you would discover whether a rupee will fall heads or tails uppermost, the money-lender will charge you less if you make an immediate experiment."'

'But how?'

'Nothing is simpler. To-morrow is Sunday. Among my little country-places there is one in the West Country which has its own cricket-field hidden in the heart of the downs. There none would see Rhodes score his century or Hugh Trumble take his hat trick. It is (as we say in Nawanagar) "not a hundred and fifty miles from here". If we start at once we could reach it by midnight, and play the great game out, single innings and to a finish, between dawn and dusk to-morrow. You will be my guests.'

'But to-morrow,' faltered F. S. Jackson, 'to-morrow is Sunday.' Cheeks blanched. Though here and there a fast bowler might be reckless and irresponsible, there was little moral turpitude among the cricketers of those days.

'Suppose,' whispered W.G., 'suppose someone got to hear of it? A cricket match on a Sunday! Why, it might even get into the papers, and then think of the harm that would be done to cricket. We may have our little squabbles, boys, but they are, after all, family quarrels. We're united at bottom. We all know we have a duty – the duty of protecting the future of the great game we love from its natural enemy: the Press gang.'

'In Nawanagar we have a proverb: "The more auspicious the day in the opinion of the most reputable sooth-sayers, the more illustrious the achievements performed upon it."'

And that was how, as the sun rose above the circle of oaks on the rolling shoulder of down above the cricket ground, the teams of England and Australia stepped forth from the finely appointed marquee above which floated the flag of Nawanagar.

The teams, I say: the teams bar one man. Ernest Jones had got separated from his Australian fellows in the dark at Didcot, and was not there when the train went out. That was that. There was no other train till Monday morning.

'Make a better game of it with us a man short,' said Joe Darling as they took the field. 'After all, it was Jonah who practically won that Nottingham match for us. You should have a very fair chance this time, W.G.'

And then there came a shout from the oak woods. Frank Iredale and Frank Laver emerged, their white boots wet with dew, the arms of one full of mushrooms, the arms of the other bearing a struggling figure in a mackintosh.

Joe Darling surveyed him. 'There's a sort of insane look about him, I should say.'

'He could easily be a Press-gang chap,' agreed W.G.

The small figure kicked and struggled, and at last fell with a thud on Laver's boot.

'I'm no journalist,' he declared with passionate sincerity. 'I'm a research chemist.'

There was a long pause.

'What would a research chemist be doing in your woods at dawn, Ranji?' asked Clement Hill in the gentle, innocent tones with which a cross-examining counsel knots the noose for a necktie party.

'Looking for moulds,' said the mackintosh. 'You take my word for it, if you can only find the right moulds you'll cure all sorts of diseases. Pneumonia and – oh lots of things.'

'He can't be very mad, he's a good throw-in,' explained Frank Iredale. 'He kept us at bay with fir-cones for a good five minutes. We thought he'd do to level up the sides.'

'All right, W.G., you can take him. That'll be twelve to ten: fair enough.'

'What's your name?'

'Adam Nyren. And may I ask who you are?'

'My name is W. G. Grace.'

'Not *Dr.* W. G. Grace?'

'Yes.'

'My dear sir, I'm delighted to meet you. I came across an interesting confinement case of yours, when you were practising in Stapleton Road in Bristol. Mrs. Larken. You sat up with her all night.'

'I remember the case perfectly. It was during a week-end when I got hundreds in both innings of a county match.'

'Really? You play first-class cricket? I play for the village – that is, whenever I can get away from mould-gathering and my laboratory.'

'You do? Then won't you join us? Mr. Darling here is a man short.'

'I should be pleased to bat and bowl you know, Mr. —er—Darling. Last Whit-Monday we played Staple Cross, and I—'

'Really? You'll field long-leg for us,' said Joe Darling. 'I don't expect we'll have to trouble you to bat. We should have won the game long before then. Never mind your clothes.'

The milk had not yet been delivered to Number 221B Baker Street, where Sherlock Holmes was busy on a problem still too delicate to be specified, when W.G. stood up majestically flourishing his bat waist-high, to await the first ball of the match from Howell. He drove this commonplace half volley into a path of nettles behind extra-cover. The second ball was a long hop. The massive drive caught it on the rise. It fluttered the tail-feathers on the first lark of the morning over the young corn behind mid-wicket.

By the time the teams adjourned for a late breakfast, 80 was on the board and the partnership was unbroken. The bowling too was running out. Laver, sprinting for a catch on the boundary, had tripped over a mole-hill and sprawled full length into a patch of nettles which had turned his right hand from a leather hip-bath into a huge, puffed, white blister. A true Australian, he had unhesitatingly offered to bowl left-handed, but, even so, his analysis had suffered.

Nor did breakfast prove to be the best change bowler in the world. C. B. Fry resumed his innings in the careless mood of a country boy flicking the heads off buttercups with a hazel twig on an afternoon walk. He played mashie shots off Noble's yorkers into the northern beetfield; mashie shots off Trumble's back-breaks into the eastern barley; mashie shots off Howell's shooters into the only nettle patch in the county which had no healing dock-leaf within sight.

As they crossed, while young Rhodes impudently rattled the tins as he put 120 on the board, Joe Darling noticed Nyren tossing the ball up to Hughie Trumble. Well! The fellow could certainly produce a break and a half. After all, it was only a sporting village ground – the fellow's own midden at that. It might be worth giving the fellow an over.

When Grace had twice pasted Trumble under his left leg to the boundary, Joe Darling threw the ball to Nyren.

'Here you, try an over at the beet-field end.'

You couldn't tell from the way the fellow placed his field quite what sort of stuff he was going to try to bowl. He had three slips, but also a couple of deep fields. He walked back very slowly to the bowler's wicket: then turned and held the ball up to his eyes. Somebody muttered that there were old prints showing bowlers of the Hambledon Club (Nyren was a name there, too) in just such an attitude. Somebody muttered back that it was older than that – probably the Druidical ritual for putting a curse on your enemy.

Then Nyren loped slowly, carelessly, up to bowl. He sent down a lazy ball that seemed innocent if straight. W.G. played his shot at it, and missed. The ball seemed to hang for a moment between sky and turf, in a state of suspense like Mohammed's coffin in the fable. Then it touched down, and slid like a snake towards the middle stump. W.G.'s size-ten boot stopped it. Time seemed to stand still.

There was not a shadow of doubt that the Champion was leg-before-wicket, as soon as anyone gave tongue in appeal. But sheer shock had struck Australia dumb. Every man on the field stood petrified – every man but Adam Nyren, who calmly walked down the pitch, recovered the ball, and went thoughtfully back to the beginning of his run. To his dying day Kelly remembered how, during those seconds when the clock of life ceased to tick, two Red Admiral butterflies, looping and tumbling above the pitch, froze in mid-air. He said afterwards that he couldn't have raised a hand to point at them for all next season's wool-clip.

As he turned to begin his run, Nyren remarked casually (his voice was sweet and clear as a choirboy's): 'I never appeal for l.b.w. After all, it's only a matter of opinion. I like the batsman to be satisfied beyond all possible doubt that he's out.'

Then the spell was broken. The whole field came alive again. The butterflies finished their loop and Adam Nyren scudded to the wicket and bowled his second ball. It was a scorcher. Charles Fry said afterwards that it was about as fast as Richardson at his best; but the Champion said no, it was quicker than that – it reminded him of Freeman of Yorkshire in the golden age before himself had bludgeoned the real fast bowlers out of the game. It pitched on the middle stump and spurned away towards the slips. W.G.'s bat waved feebly at it and a click sounded clear as a pizzicato note on the violin.

Kelly crouched and caught: and up shot the ball from his gloves and the triumph-shout from his lips. It was echoed in the slips and at square leg. It was echoed, one regrets to say, at long-off, where Clem Hill thought that nothing should be left to chance. Every voice shot up: but the umpire's fingers remained clenched in his pocket. It was all very well trusting to the evidence of one's own ears, but what about when these suggested that the Champion could be caught at the wicket off a tyro without having scored a single run off him? In the interests of justice it was his clear duty to disbelieve these untrustworthy members. Besides, if he hadn't, it was doubtful whether the Old Man would ever recommend him for a Gentlemen and Players match again.

The third ball of that famous over was very short. It pitched little more than half-way to the batsman and broke hugely away to the off. W.G., joyous as a pirate at an execution, lunged at it and missed. Under his bat the ball landed second bounce – and cut away almost at right angles in an off-break. Frank Iredale swore he heard the leg stump give a sigh as it sank back to mother earth.

Nobody dared to clap. Then Nyren said: 'A fluke, really. I can't always guarantee that one will come off.'

There was everything daunting in K. S. Ranjitsinhiji's walk to the wicket. It was soundless and full of menace: a panther stepping up to the spring. There, too, at the far end, waited the other half of the formidable partnership – the calm and dominating Fry. In many minds memories floated like summer shadows across the green morning: memories of Yorkshire wilting, of Lancashire bowlers stewed and suffering, of proud Kent hobbling defeated out of Canterbury before indestructible Sussex. Guard given, Ranji adjusted his Crusader's cap and glanced over his shoulder to make sure the famous leg-glide would be out of reach of the fleetest fine-leg.

'I'll try my fast ball,' Nyren murmured from the end of his run like a child speaking in his innocent sleep. He ambled gently up to the wicket and rolled his arm sleepily over – the sort of action behind which in a more sophisticated age Hearne the Younger masked the lethal googly.

Ranji, fanning the square-leg umpire (knocked out by a flying bail), was heard to say that he never saw the ball from the moment it left the bowler's hand, though he admitted to hearing something that sounded like the whizz of a very large bullet. He good-naturedly joined in the search for the fragments of the middle stump and the attempt to reconstitute it, before retiring in a brown study to the pavilion.

In the train on the journey down, the Honourable F. S. Jackson had confided to Charles Fry: 'It's a curious thing, at the beginning of an innings I'm always nervous that someone will conjure me out with one of these fancy leg-breaks before my eye's in. But the moment they send me down an honest yorker my nerve comes back. I see the ball as big as a football – I'm in control.'

Adam Nyren skimmed off the Hon. F. S. Jackson's bail first ball, with a yorker.

As the field changed ends, Nyren, with a mysterious air, approached Joe Darling. 'Forgive me mentioning it,' he said, 'but I think there's a good chance of a collapse. If you'd let me have another over or two, I believe we might yet get them on the run.'

He was given his chance. The third ball of his second over produced the first run off the bowling. William Gunn jerked his body out of danger of a fast break-back, and the ball trickled off the edge of his bat towards long leg. The batsmen raced across, and as Charles Fry grounded his bat the players in the pavilion began to cheer as they would have cheered a double century. Even the fieldsmen started to clap. Gunn, stiff as a ramrod, removed his cap and solemnly acknowledged the ovation. But the rest of the over was on normal lines. Fry was bowled by the fourth ball, but returned elated by the fact that he had had all three stumps knocked clean out of the ground. It seemed to give him a sort of standing among the damned.

Tom Hayward, too, died happy in Nyren's third over. He was, indeed, out for a duck; but at least he was caught and bowled. Not to have been clean bowled had by now become an achievement, and when J. T. Tyldesley walked back to the tent after his first ball, he was received in silence, despite his vain-glorious mutter that he had played on.

Nyren's fourth over was less dramatic. It was true that he sent Storer's leg bail 72 paced yards from the wicket, breaking the record Mold had set up at the Oval three years previously, though nobody bothered to applaud such a perfunctory achievement. But Hirst and Rhodes were still at the wicket at the over's end, and had even increased the score by three. It was a mere flash in the pan. The next over saw Hirst's off stump cartwheeling past third man, and the leg stump shoot up like a champagne cork behind J. T. Hearne. That was that. The innings was over. Australia was set 102 runs to win.

As the fielding side moved like sleep-walkers into the tent for lunch, a great rainstorm fell out of the blue sky, and for half an hour the dazzling rainbow that spanned downland and forest was slashed by dagger strokes of forked lightning.

Then the storm was turned off like a tap. The thunder rumbled like an express train over the rain-blotted rim of the southern horizon. The sky was an unflawed sapphire horizon. Thrushes hopped about the outfield sucking up worms for all the world like lunchers in Mr. Gatti's new restaurant sucking up spaghetti.

W.G. gazed out from the door of the marquee. 'I think we can begin again at once, Joe. The outfield's perfectly safe – supposing for the moment that any of your batsmen are capable of hitting the ball so far.'

'Don't you think the ball will be rather too slippery for your bowlers to be able to get a grip on it?' asked Joe Darling solicitously.

'Oh, we'll risk it,' W.G. volunteered magnanimously, one small bright eye cocked on Wilfred Rhodes. On this wicket Rhodes would be making the ball cut through, or stand up and hiss like a snake.

The umpires led the way to the middle. Somewhere above the little oak wood a cuckoo mocked Joe Darling and every brazen hero of his team. They feared neither man nor devil, but only the black magic of an English sticky wicket. 'You're not meant to play cricket on turf like that,' muttered Syd Gregory. 'The unnatural stuff should never be disturbed – except to bury suicides in.'

And now Wilfred Rhodes was playing on this strip of earth as Paganini played on his violin. He fiddled dark masterpieces upon it: death marches, and unhallowed last rites rose like a poisonous miasma from the green grass steaming in the June sunlight.

First slip gathered up the ball from Darling's purely reflex action, aimed to protect his right eye. 'If it had been my left eye I'd never have bothered,' he muttered in defence.

The proud Trumper, alone among Australians a master on a bowler's wicket, was caught and bowled off a stroke with which schoolboys defend their shins at French cricket.

Rhodes was a Tamberlaine: Hirst a Napoleon. Only Iredale rode the whirlwind. Fast-footed and white-lipped he counter-attacked with lightning strokes for a while. He had scored 33 (several of them from the middle of his bat) before a gigantic lunge towards mid-off was comfortably caught at square-leg.

When the eighth wicket fell and Bill Howell joined Kelly, 62 runs were still needed. Joe Darling's eyes were tight closed in prayer for rain – nothing less than a monsoon would do. He only learned the worst when Bill Howell's gnarled hand clutched his shoulder and his hoarse voice muttered inadequate apology into his ear. Then he opened his eyes, and like the sportsman he was, took Bill's hand in his own.

'It doesn't matter, Bill,' he said in unfaltering tones. 'It couldn't matter less.' (Grammarians believe this to have been the first occasion on which this now household phrase was used.) 'It couldn't matter less, Bill,' said stout Joe Darling. 'After all, it's only a game.' (It was the occasion, too, of the coining of this phrase: which, in Australia, at least, has never caught on.)

Meanwhile, out in the middle a buzz went up. J. J. Kelly had played a maiden over from George Hirst. Adam Nyren, last man in, was preparing to take guard – and W.G. had taken the ball.

There was, try as he might to disguise it, a look of grim satisfaction on the face of the Champion. Vengeance was his. The gods would not, after all, allow a good man to be mocked to the end. He bowled an exquisitely flighted leg-break that kicked like an Army mule from the gluey turf. As he saw it rise and gnash its cruel teeth at the batsman, a tender look softened the fierce old face; if only old Arthur Shrewsbury had been there to be c Tyldesley b Grace by that nonpareil of a ball! How that great batsman would have esteemed the privilege of getting out to such a masterpiece! How he would have bragged, in his gentle way, for seasons on end of the delectable death-stroke the Champion had devised for him. The benevolence was somewhat abruptly wiped from W.G.'s face by the sight of Adam Nyren punching the unplayable ball in a screaming straight drive that came to earth in the heart of the beet-field beyond long-off.

The second ball he hooked out of the ground into the young corn. (W.G. doubted whether his bat was quite straight.)

The third imperiously carried the covers – a rocketing shot.

But the worst of all was the fourth ball. Straight and fast and true it was; and Nyren, with wrists like a steel-spring, cut it clear of the slips to the boundary. The whole field clapped.

'Why are you clapping?' demanded W.G. in an indignant squeal.

'It wasn't a six,' explained F. S. Jackson. 'It was only a four.'

After that the end was mercifully swift. Five more overs saw the sixty-two runs leeway dwindle to six: Nyren 49 not out, Kelly 7 not out.

Rhodes was England's last hope. W.G. put him on again. His first ball, full of malice and cunning, was majestically off-driven for four.

Two to get: two to get! W.G. remembered Cobden's Over – these great occasions had a knack of repeating themselves. Wilfred had one up his sleeve. Now, at zero-hour, at this flash-point of crisis, experience always told. This was when sophistication counted for everything. After all, Rhodes had some of these touchstone qualities – more at least than his enemy.

And then Rhodes bowled. He bowled a very bad ball: an arrant long-hop. It came easily to the bat, and Nyren played at it the one rank-bad stroke of his innings – a feeble, unforceful, uppish square-cut which lobbed, gently as a cup of tea on a tray, to W.G. at point.

'Come for one!' shouted Nyren. W.G. folded his infallible hands over the ball as it fell, and indulged the little gesture of skying the captive into mid-air. Only there was no captive to sky. The ball had fallen between his hands and lay there staring at him from the grass.

'Come again!' screamed Nyren from the far end. Kelly turned and sprinted.

There were not two runs in the stroke – there was not one. W.G. lumbered down on the ball, pulled himself up, and shied for the wicket. He missed by a foot, and Nyren ran in with his bat waving high, like a banner. The ball flashed to the boundary and disappeared into the long grass. No one ever saw it again.

That was that: Australia had won by one wicket. . . .

In the pavilion the council sat long, while, near the scoring-board, Rhodes (still young enough to live down the past) poured tea into Nyren's cup.

'There's no doubt about it, Joe,' F. S. Jackson murmured, 'Australia's won her last Test Match for as long as you or I will be playing. This fellow can't be twenty-five. Until he retires you've no hope of holding your own.'

Joe Darling pondered. 'W.G.,' he said.

'Well?'

'Remember what you said – good lord, was it only yesterday? It seems like centuries ago.'

'What did I say?'

'Something about cricket being greater than us all. That we might have our quarrels, but they were only family squabbles: we were all together in wanting to keep our great game whole and healthy.'

'So I did. Well?'

'If this chap plays, *will* cricket be whole and healthy? Will there be any cricket ever again? Won't there just be Adam Nyren, and a—a—chorus, a line of fellows walking on?'

'Or walking off.'

'Exactly. Would it be——' Joe Darling drew a deep breath and coined a phrase which has been revived from time to time by subsequent orators, 'Would it be – cricket?'

'I see what you mean.'

'One thing,' said the voice of the youngest in council, 'the public would never take the least interest in any of *us* ever again. We'd never get *our* pictures in the newspapers. No more small boys would rush in droves after you down St. John's Wood Road, W.G., vying for the honour of carrying your cricket bag.'

'Poof-poof! What does that matter? The point is, *would* it be good for cricket?'

There was a pause unusually long even considering that this was a cricketers' conversation.

'You're right, Joe. He must never play again.'

'But what are we to do with him? How can we stop him?'

Again the shadows passed across the green field outside. Rhodes refilled the tea cup. In the pavilion no one spoke.

Then:

'We might pack him off to Yorkshire.'

'What would be the good of that, Jackson?'

'It would be good-bye to his chance of playing first-class cricket. Lord Hawke doesn't allow it: unless you're Yorkshire-born. Except, of course,' he added fairly, 'in his own case. One must admit that *he* was born in Lincolnshire.'

'There is a sinister fellow in Nawanagar who is said to get wonderful results by sticking pins into clay statues made to scale. Needless to say, I don't believe in such things. All he needs is a hair belonging to his—er—client.'

'A friend of mine has a useful little gold mine. It's called Broken Hill. I'm sure he'd give it to the fellow if I asked him. It would keep him occupied for years.'

The suggestions flocked in, thick and fast as the swallows jinking hard-winged through the midsummer evening outside the tent. At last Joe Darling cried: 'The time – the time! We shall miss our train.'

'That would never do. We have to keep faith with the public tomorrow. Well, I suppose the best thing will be, W.G., for you to take him home with you and keep him under your eye until we decide.'

'Very well. By the way, before we break up——'

It was at this stage, it is believed, that the oath of silence was enjoined, if such an oath, rather than the failing memories of the ageing survivors of this game, is indeed responsible for the paucity of detail in the hands of historians.

The cricketers tramped out on to the lane, W.G. and Adam Nyren leading the way.

And then – in a flash – it happened. A thunderbot from Jove could not have been more sudden or (even in the light of all that Sabbath-breaking) more unexpected.

But this was no thunderbolt. It came with a reek of paraffin and a clash of machinery, not from above but from round a hairpin bend, where high banks concealed the road from the driver of the 7 h.p. de Dion Bouton, gaze he never so intently through his goggles.

There was a clank and a jangle and a crash. The goggles were cracked – flying splinters of glass strewed the road. At least five of the seven horses animating the machine appeared to have pulled up. Then the wheels pawed the air in the ditch – and Adam Nyren lay slumped in the middle of a road which had never before been trodden by solid Dunlop tyres.

It was Joe Darling (with W.G.) who carried him back into the marquee and laid him reverently on the long trestle table.

'Is there any hope?' gulped Joe Darling. 'Is there any hope at all – Dr. Grace?'

'His heart is still beating. We may not be too late.'

'What can you do?'

'Do? Why, operate at once, of course. It's the only chance. Fortunately I carry my doctor's bag with me wherever I go. Indeed, I've managed to make room for a special place for it in my cricket bag. Here we are now! Turn him over Joe. That's right. . . . Gently . . . gently. . . .'

The clouds had gathered over the splendour of the June evening when the flaps of the tent were pushed aside, and Grace and Darling stepped forth to join the silent host of men with paper-white faces huddled on the edge of the field. It was the driver of the car himself who flung forward, shudderingly, like a man reeling under drink, to mumble his question.

'You have – you have operated?'

'Yes, indeed.'

'And the operation——?'

'The operation was a success.'

W.G. raised his red-and-yellow cricket cap reverently high above his head. The two teams fell into step and followed him to the station.

THAT is the story, built from its essentials, which I heard from my friend in the sports-shop in Hastings in 1938.

What happened to Nyren? W. G. Grace saved his life, but his hip-bone had been badly broken, and it never set properly. He couldn't play cricket again. A curious further result of the accident was that his concussion wiped out for ever his memory of that single day. He took to following first-class cricket in the newspapers later in his life (I discovered), and, when W.G. died, Nyren was heard to say that he wished he had seen the Champion play.

There remains the question of how my friend at Hastings got the details of the match. He gave them to me as an eye-witness account. Myself, I wonder still about the other umpire, not yet accounted for. I haven't tried to tie up the loose ends, but Ranji was a Sussex man. Perhaps that second umpire was a young man on Ranji's estate. Perhaps Ranji bought his silence (in an English way) by setting him up behind the Marine Parade in a small shop, and himself footed the bill for the first stock of bat-oil, plimsolls and chest-expanders. I don't know.

But I know one man who does know. That's Charles Fry. I've tried to get him talking about it, at Lord's, at the Savile, in Brown's Hotel. But a far-away look comes into that mild and magnificent eye, and he says he never plays cricket on Sundays. It's not quite good enough.

Short Story, *1948*

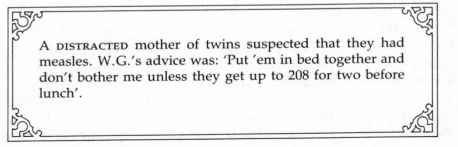

A DISTRACTED mother of twins suspected that they had measles. W.G.'s advice was: 'Put 'em in bed together and don't bother me unless they get up to 208 for two before lunch'.

A Day of Grace

GEORGE MARVILL

ONCE upon a time country cricket matches were played from Monday to Wednesday and from Thursday to Saturday. In those days of old-fashioned summers and brisker cricket a match begun on Thursday would often finish before lunch on Saturday. On Saturday mornings, among the crowd at the county ground, there would be a number of purposeful-looking men glaring intently at the field, with an occasional eye on the clock. They were the delegates from local cricket clubs – village, chapel, and working-men's – charged by their committees with the task of ensnaring a star player and bringing him home with them to play in the afternoon match.

Thus it happened that at about 1.30 p.m. on a sunny Saturday long ago my Great-uncle William drove into Eckerslyke in Councillor Cakebread's gig, bearing as captive a burly, impressively bewhiskered and on the whole quite good-humoured giant, at the sight of whom a tremendous cheer went up from the Eckerslykians thronging the High Street. Nobody recalls now by what blandishments Dr. W. G. Grace was induced to come out to Eckerslyke to play for Eckerslyke Wesleyans in their match with Gawmston Primitives; it is undeniably a fact that he came. The Gawmston Primitives were dismayed when they saw him standing with Councillor Cakebread in the centre of the field, blandly surveying an admiring crowd several times larger than the average gate in the Nonconformist League.

Dawson Wolfenden, the Gawmston captain, drew Great-uncle William aside. 'Fair's fair, tha knaws, William,' he said. 'Our chaps sud be given some sooart of a chance to keep in t' running for t' Cup.' Great-uncle William, who was the Eckerslyke Wesleyans' captain, filled his pipe and said nothing. 'What I'm trying to tell tha,' went on Dawson, 'is, tha owt to keep Grace off bowling altogether. Tha can let him bat if tha likes. But let our chaps knock a few up for thersens – don't let 'em be put to rout altogether.'

'Well, by gow!' said Great-uncle William. 'What does ta think all these fowk are here for? They've come to watch Grace, not thee.'

Great-uncle William ultimately promised to keep Grace in hand as his first change-bowler. As it happened he did not have to call on 'W.G.' at all in that innings, Gawmston batted first and were all out for 27 to Eckerslyke's opening bowlers. Perhaps the Primitives were hypnotized by that huge bear-like figure crouching in the slips and chewing nonchalantly at a straw. Most of them, at least, kept their eyes on 'W.G.'

instead of the bowler, and four of them, almost with an air of being anxious to oblige, scooped their first ball obediently into his capacious hands.

'W.G.' opened the batting for Eckerslyke Wesleyans, and seemed all set to knock up the required 28 and a good many more – until his partner's wicket fell with the score at eighteen and Ezra Hardcastle came out to bat. Ezra was a sour, suspicious, wizened little man, in whom it was notoriously difficult to induce a willing suspension of disbelief. At the weekly meeting of the cricket committee he opposed any measures which seemed to promise a departure from the ordinary; he taunted Great-uncle William, who usually sponsored such proposals, with being 'too big for his booits.' He had jeered at the committee's decision to invite Grace to play. When Great-uncle William, pointing to his prize, said: 'Nah then, tha sees, we've gotten him,' Ezra replied, 'Tha's gotten somebody that lewks like him, tha means.' Great-uncle William was to remember this later, and for a long time to come.

Ezra, as was his cautious wont, stonewalled the rest of the over. When 'W.G.' faced the bowling he flicked the second ball past the slips and began to run. Ezra stood stock-still, shouting 'Get back!' 'Come on, man!' bellowed 'W.G.,' still advancing. 'We can make it two if you look alive!'

Ezra refused to budge. The situation rapidly became tragic; he and the irate 'W.G.' were together at the bowling end. The wicket-keeper, to whom the ball had been quickly returned, danced with joy at the prospect of the so-distinguished wicket fallen into his hands. 'How's that?' he inquired gleefully removing the bails.

The umpire – it was the Eckerslyke umpire – said 'Out.' 'Well, by —!' said 'W.G.', regarding Ezra with disgust. He began to stride towards the pavilion. 'Not thee,' said the umpire. 'It's Ezra that's out.'

'W.G.' pulled up, amazed. A stunned silence pervaded the field, the verdict was so outrageously in flat contradiction of all known rulings. 'Gerraway!' said Ezra at last. 'How can I be out? It's him that left his crease, not me!' 'Tha's out, Ah tells tha,' said the umpire. 'Off tha goes.'

A hostile murmur began to swell from the Gawmston supporters. A few influential Eckerslykians were scratching their heads ruefully. Ezra might have had the support of both sides had he not said and done a blasphemous thing. 'It's my belief yon chap's nowt but an impostor,' he said. 'Does ta think W. G. Grace 'ud come out to play for a tuppenny-hawpenny team like Eckerslyke, and then run hisself out like this feller's done? Watch here, sitha.' He reached up to the colossal beard, flourishingly menacingly above him, and gave it a mighty tug.

The spectators gulped. The beard remained firm. 'Tha's out now,' said the umpire, 'if tha warn't afore – making a public nuisance o' thysen on t' field.' Ezra gazed about him, reading horror on every face, and began to feel a little frightened at what he had done. 'T' chap could still be an impostor, couldn't he, even if t' beard's genuine?' he objected. 'Anyhow, tha's welcome to him.' Even the Gawmston Primitives forebore to protest as Ezra walked away.

The bearded batsman – it was W. G. Grace, of course, as old men in the West Riding will tell you to this day – stayed to bring the Eckerslyke Wesleyans' score to 150 for six, of which he made 100 not out. The Gawmston Primitives were sent in again, and were all out for 24, Grace taking six of their wickets for nine runs.

MANCHESTER GUARDIAN, *Monday 5 August 1957*

— 14 —

A MOVE TO ELYSIAN FIELDS

W.G.

ALPHA OF THE PLOUGH (A. G. GARDINER)

THE worst of spending week-ends in the country in these anxious days is the difficulty of getting news. About six o'clock on Saturday evening I am seized with a furious hunger. What has happened on the East front? What on the West? What in Serbia? Has Greece made up its heroic mind? Is Rumania still trembling on the brink? What does the French communiqué say? These and a hundred other questions descend on me with frightful insistence. Clearly I can't go to bed without having them answered. But there is not an evening paper to be got nearer than the little railway station in the valley two miles away, and there is no way of getting it except by Shanks' mare. And so, unable to resist the glamour of *The Star*, I start out across the fields for the station.

As I stood on the platform last Saturday evening devouring the latest war news under the dim oil lamp, a voice behind me said, in broad rural accent, 'Bill, I say, W.G. is dead.' At the word I turned hastily to another column and found the news that had stirred him. And even in the midst of world-shaking events it stirred me too. For a brief moment I forgot the war and was back in that cheerful world where we used to be happy, where we greeted the rising sun with light hearts and saw its setting without fear. In that cheerful world I can hardly recall a time when a big man with a black beard was not my King.

I first saw him in the 'seventies. I was a small boy then, and I did him the honour of playing truant – 'playing wag' we called it. I felt that the occasion demanded it. To have the god of my idolatry in my own little town and not to pay him my devotions – why, the idea was almost like blasphemy. A half-dozen, or even a dozen, from my easily infuriated master would be a small price to pay. I should take the stripes as a homage to the hero. He would never know, but I should be proud to suffer in his honour. Unfortunately there was a canvas round the field where the hero played, and as the mark of the Mint was absent from my pockets I was on the wrong side of the canvas. But I knew a spot where by lying flat on your stomach and keeping your head very low you could see under the canvas and get a view of the wicket. It was not a comfortable position, but I saw the King. I think I was a little disappointed that there was nothing supernatural about his appearance and that there were no portents in the heavens to announce his coming. It didn't seem quite right somehow. In a general way I knew he was only a man, but I was quite prepared to see something tremendous happen, the sun to dance or the earth to heave, when he appeared. I never felt the indifference of Nature to the affairs of men so acutely.

I saw him many times afterwards, and I suppose I owe more undiluted happiness to him than to any man that ever lived. For he was the genial tyrant in a world that was all sunshine. There are other games, no doubt, which will give you as much exercise and pleasure in playing them as cricket, but there is no game that fills the mind with such memories and seems enveloped in such a gracious and kindly atmosphere. If you have once loved it and played it, you will find talk in it enough 'for the wearing out of six fashions', as Falstaff says. I like a man who has cricket in his soul. I find I am prejudiced in his favour, and am disposed to disbelieve any ill about him. I think my affection for Jorkins began with the discovery that he, like myself, saw that astounding catch with which Ulyett dismissed Bonnor in the Australian match at Lord's in 1883 – or was it 1884? And when to this mutual and immortal memory we added the discovery that we were both at the Oval at the memorable match when Crossland rattled Surrey out like ninepins and the crowd mobbed him, and Key and Roller miraculously pulled the game out of the fire, our friendship was sealed.

The fine thing about a wrangle on cricket is that there is no bitterness in it. When you talk about politicians you are always on the brink of bad temper. When you disagree about the relative merits of W. B. Yeats or Francis Thompson you are afflicted with scorn for the other's lack of perception. But you may quarrel about cricketers and love each other all the time. For example, I am prepared to stand up in a truly Christian spirit to the bowling of anybody in defence of my belief that – next to him of the black beard – Lohmann was the most naturally gifted all-round cricketer there has ever been. What grace of action he had, what an instinct for the weak spot of his opponent, what a sense for fitting the action to the moment, above all, what a gallant spirit he played the game in! And that, after all, is the real test of the great cricketer. It is the man who brings the spirit of adventure into the game that I want. Of the Quaifes and the Scottons and the Barlows I have nothing but dreary memories. They do not mean cricket to me. And even Shrewsbury and Hayward left me cold. They were too faultily faultless, too icily regular for my taste. They played cricket not as though it was a game, but as though it was a proposition in Euclid. And I don't like Euclid.

It was the hearty joyousness that 'W.G.' shed around him that made him so dear to us youngsters of all ages. I will admit, if you like, that Ranjitsinhji at his best was more of a magician with the bat, that Johnny Briggs made you laugh more with his wonderful antics, that A. P. Lucas had more finish, Palairet more grace, and so on. But it was the abundance of the old man with the black beard that was so wonderful. You never came to the end of him. He was like a generous roast of beef – you could cut and come again, and go on coming. Other men flitted across our sky like meteors, but he shone on like the sun in the heavens, and like the sun in the heavens he scattered largesse over the land. He did not seem so much a man as an institution, a symbol of summer and all its joys, a sort of Father Christmas clothed in flannels and sunshine. It did you good merely to look at him. It made you feel happy to see such a huge capacity for enjoyment, such mighty subtlety, such ponderous gaiety. It was as though Jove, or Vulcan, or some other god of antiquity had come down to play games with the mortals. You would not have been much surprised if, when the shadows lengthened across the greensward and the umpire signalled that the day's play was done, he had wrapped himself in a cloud of glory and floated away to Olympus.

And now he is gone indeed, and it seems as though a part, and that a very happy part, of my life has gone with him. When sanity returns to the earth, there will arise other deities of the cricket field, but not for me. Never again shall I recapture the careless rapture that came with the vision of the yellow cap flaming above the black beard, of the Herculean frame and the mighty bared arms, and all the godlike apparition of the master. As I turned out of the little station and passed through the fields and climbed the hill I felt that the darkness that has come upon the earth in these days had taken a deeper shade of gloom, for even the lights of the happy past were being quenched.

PEBBLES ON THE SHORE, *Dent, 1916*

G. K. CHESTERTON once said that Pickwick was the true English fairy, and W.G., that bulky sprite, was a prodigious Puck in a truly mid-summer's day dream.

The First German War

CLIFFORD BAX

HE PLAYED his last game of big cricket in 1908, but he still turned out occasionally in local matches – and what a stir he must have made among the onlookers, what awe he must have aroused in the changing room . . . If the First German War (1914–18) had not occurred, he might have continued until he was seventy to teach the Young Idea how to bat. He played for the very last time in a match between Eltham and Grove Park on July the 25th, 1914. According to Mr. Darwin 'he made 31 runs on a fiery and impossible wicket, and the last bowlers who ever bowled to him could not get him out'. The Editor of *Wisden* (1949) states, however, that 'he scored 69 not out in a total of 155 for six wickets . . .' and I assume that we must accept *Wisden* as gospel-truth.

Who can doubt that he would have batted on several other occasions during that fateful August if Germany had been less overweening? As it was, he wrote a letter to *The Sportsman* proposing that the first-class cricket-season should be guillotined. He may never before have 'written to the papers', and it may have been that letter which did abruptly close the championship contest, for in those happier days a great many Britons still thought of any war as a purely professional affair. In his letter he said, 'It is not fitting at a time like the present that able-bodied men should play day after day and pleasure-seekers look on. There are so many who are young and able and yet are hanging back. I should like to see all first-class cricketers of suitable age, set a good example, and come to the help of their country without delay in its hour of need.' Even so he might have been gratified if he had seen Mr. C. O. H. Sewell, playing for Gloucestershire at the Oval a few days before 'the end', smite the Surrey bowlers with a fierce abandon and score 165; but he was not present or we should certainly have marked him, for that beard would have been visible across the whole breadth of the Oval.

Grace had now retired and was financially at ease; but the war troubled him. No man of his own period ever expected Great Britain to be involved in a dangerous war, or at least not after the French scare in the 'seventies . . . In 1915, came the Zeppelin and aeroplane raids on England – presumably including Bristol. They now seem few and strangely ineffectual. They were, nevertheless, a danger which had only been imagined for a few years; and we are told that they alarmed W.G. to a surprising degree. He must have been a brave man. Perhaps it will sound fantastic to compare the perils of an air-raid with the perils of batting against fast bowlers on an untamed wicket, and yet we should remember that Freeman, referring to a match played in 1870, observed, 'Tom Emmett and I have often said it was a marvel that the Doctor was not either maimed or unnerved for the rest of his days, or killed outright . . . A modern batsman,' he continued, 'should have seen our expresses flying about his ribs, shoulders and head in 1870.' In a word he dreaded those aerial attacks because no bat could counter them.

He spent much time in his garden, possibly encouraging the asparagus beds, and certainly attending with minute care to his putting-green. His practice on it was so assiduous that he became an admirable putter in match-play. No doubt (since he had so little taste for reading) he beguiled the evenings over whist with old and new cronies. It was in the garden on a day of October that W.G., aged sixty-seven, had a stroke, and of course he must have recognized that danger-signal. He got back to the house, and they put him to bed. His distress was soon over for he died on the 23rd. October the 26th was a fierce day but in the afternoon, war or no war, the church at Elmers End 'was filled to overflowing and, at the conclusion of the first portion of the service, the lengthy procession of mourners made their way to the grave, where the hero of cricket was laid to rest beside a son and daughter who had preceded him into the Land of Shadows' (*Memorial Biography*).

It is surprising, despite the tremendous actions in France, that *Punch* did not permit himself to mourn Grace in a full-page cartoon. It is no less surprising that its half-page valedictory to so typical an Englishman should seem tepid and unworthy, for we learn from the *Memorial Biography* that it was written by E. V. Lucas, a skilled essayist and a fanatical lover of cricket. Those who knew Lucas will be disappointed to find that he encouraged the belief that W.G. did little doctoring; affirms that Grace called that short ball on the leg-side 'my bread-and-butter trick'; and did no better in his peroration than to say 'towards the last he might almost have been a work of Mestrovic, so colossal and cosmic were his lines. Peace to his ashes! We shall never look upon his like again. The days of Grace are ended.' The Bishop of Hereford (before Grace had died) did much better, saying at a banquet, 'Had he been born in ancient Greece the *Iliad* would have been a different book. Had he lived in the Middle Ages, he would have been a Crusader and would now have been lying with his legs crossed in some ancient abbey, having founded a great family.' Better still are the verses by D. L. A. Jephson, the Surrey captain and almost the last of our lob-bowlers:

> With what great zest through all your merry years,
> Did you not cast into a million hearts
> The golden spirit of our English game,

To hearts that otherwise had passed it by!
Dead; and from Death a myriad memories rise
Deathless; we thank you, friend, that once you lived.

This may be the only example of a cricket poem in blank verse. It was no occasion for a hopping jingle.

W. G. GRACE, CRICKETING LIVES, *Phoenix House*, 1952

Epilogue

A. A. THOMSON

THE cemetery chapel was packed with mourners, most of them cricketers, in or out of uniform. There they were, the men bred in Gloucestershire: J. A. Bush, the wicketkeeper who had been his best man, O. G. Radcliffe, who had shared many partnerships with him, R. F. Miles, Frank Townsend and the rest of them. With them was C. E. Green, who had played for several counties and a year before had proudly proposed his health. There was the Jam Sahib of Nawanagar, once known as Ranji and now in staff officer's uniform, and with him were those civilians in khaki, P. F. Warner, H. D. G. Leveson-Gower and the Somersetshire hitter, H. T. Hewett. Many professionals were there too: not those rugged warriors of W.G.'s golden days, James Shaw, Fred Morley, Tom Emmett and Happy Jack Ulyett, for they had died before him. These were the working cricketers of a later time: Alec Hearne, Huish, the Kent wicketkeeper; Martin, the left-hand bowler who had rattled the Australians in 1890; Razor Smith ('I always knew you were a fool') and Philip Need, the Lord's dressing-room attendant, whose benefit match was the last in which W.G. had turned out to play.

When the procession wound from the chapel to the graveside, the massive coffin was followed by members of the family, by C. L. Townsend, most brilliantly apt of the Old Man's cricketing pupils, and by Lord Hawke and Lord Harris, those two great captains of the north and south, who had been his admiring coevals and were to live on into an age that knew not Grace.

They laid him under a hawthorn tree. There are other trees nearby: a horse-chestnut behind and a sycamore on the right. In fifty years of sun and rain they have grown in girth and spread their branches. On that melancholy day they looked shabby and forlorn. Ended was cricket's great age in which he had played and laughed with schoolboy gusto.

And as that great company melted away into the darkening shadows of the October evening, there was hardly one among them who could fully realize the bitter truth: never again would they hear that jolly high-pitched chuckle or see that mighty figure at the crease.

> From quiet homes and first beginning
> Out to the undiscovered ends,
> There's nothing worth the wear of winning
> But laughter and the love of friends.

The laughter was stilled. The love of friends, valiant and abiding, remained and will remain as long and 'as sure as God's in Gloucestershire'.

Many a man felt that his king was gone. A friend of mine was in France, as most of us were in those days. The night before he was due to come home on leave he dreamed, without any apparent reason, of W.G. When he reached London, he heard that W.G. was dead and that the funeral was to take place the following day. A strong feeling impelled him to go down past the old Crystal Palace, which war had turned into a naval establishment, to the cemetery at Elmers End. There he joined the melancholy cavalcade at the graveside and as the mourners finally melted away into the cold, autumnal twilight, he lingered for a moment near the grave. There he stood and, perhaps because he was of an old-fashioned schoolmasterly type, brought up on the Victorian poets, there ran, or rather marched through his mind – absurdly, perhaps, but sadly – the slow, melancholy music of Tennyson's 'Morte d'Arthur'. He saw himself – yes, of course, it was absurd – as Sir Bedivere, watching with a sick heart the passing of the great King.

> 'This day unsolders all the goodliest fellowship
> Whereof this world holds record . . .'

He pondered on the fevered and sombre picture of the war and its dark menace of worse to come; it might be that the old peaceful days of leisure and pleasure in the green fields of England would never come again. . . . The poem was still in his mind; he thought of the vaguely noble figure of King Arthur, the misty shadow of a poet's dream; and he thought of the wholly different 'king' who lay there in the still open grave but a few yards away, who had been so robust, so earthy, so richly endowed, not poetically, but in flesh and blood, in his own 'big assemblance', with the spirit of English laughter and the summer country scene. For an instant he thought he heard a friendly shout –

Returning from the nets during a game between Mr Stoddart's XI and the Rest of England, 5–7 September 1898, Hastings (*Roger Mann Collection*)

Hastings again three years later. This time it is an England XI (*v.* Yorkshire). *Back row* (L to R); A. Shaw (umpire), Lilley, Vine, Hayward, J.T. Tyldesley, Field, Abel, Jas. Lillywhite (umpire). *Front row*: Jessop, Ranjitsinhji, W.G., A.O. Jones, Mason. A formidable team (*Roger Mann Collection*)

Collecting for Belgian Refugees, Catford Bridge, 1915. Looks like A.C. MacLaren on the left, Grace's successor as England captain (*Roger Mann Collection*)

L to R: nephew of Ranji's (not Duleepsinhji), A.C. MacLaren, W.G., Ranjitsinhji, W.G. Heasman. In Grace's garden, *c.* 1915 (MCC Library)

'Don't like those damned Doodlebugs.' One of the last, if not the last, picture of Grace outside his front door at Fairmount, Mottingham (*Roger Mann Collection*)

'There will never be another not only to play cricket as Grace did, but to be cricket as Grace was' (E.V. Lucas). The final resting place at Elmers End, under threat from a proposed road scheme (*MCC Library*)

IN TENDER MEMORY
OF
BESSIE
THE DEARLY LOVED
AND ONLY DAUGHTER OF

WILLIAM GILBERT & AGNES NICHOLLS
GRACE
BORN MAY 28TH 1878
DIED FEBRUARY 6TH 1899.

ALSO OF WILLIAM GILBERT GRACE,
THEIR DEARLY LOVED ELDEST SON,
BORN JULY 6TH 1874, DIED MARCH 2ND 1905.
"BLESSED ARE THE PURE IN HEART: FOR THEY SHALL SEE GOD."
ALSO OF WILLIAM GILBERT GRACE,
BORN JULY 18TH 1848, DIED OCTOBER 23RD 1915.

THE DEARLY LOVED HUSBAND OF AGNES NICHOLLS GRACE.
WHO ALSO RESTS HERE
BORN AUGUST 3RD 1853–DIED MARCH 23RD 1930.

A succinct letter from Walter Mead (Essex, London County, England) to John Arlott. What more is there to say? (*Roger Mann Collection*)

Dear Sir
My Opinion of W. G. Grace he was a very great cricketer
W. mead

'Well cot, oh, well cot!' – and the grave enunciation of first principles:
'I'd say you ought to put the bat against the ba . . . all . . .'

The leaves of the three nearby trees had nearly all gone, but in the
gathering dusk a light wind swayed their branches. On the wind there
came to his imagination a whisper, faint but growing, and somehow it
seemed that in the whisper was a promise – a promise that 'the goodliest
fellowship' would never be finally unsoldered, and that, despite war
and winter, summer's world of happy days would come again, would
always come again. . . . He walked down the curved path into the broad
walk towards the gate. It was almost dark. The wind was still blowing
and in the sound of it the end-line of the poem swelled like a
trumpet-call:

> And the new sun rose, bringing the new year.

THE GREAT CRICKETER, *Hale, 1957*

'To W. G. Grace'

WELL done, Leviathan! We send thee here
   A birthday greeting for thy jubilee;
Unparalleled in scoring, now this year
   Another half hundred brings to thee.
Straight as thy bat has been thy course in life
   And still thy force unwasted forward plays;
Thy splendid vigour with decay holds strife,
   And Time, that runs out all, with thee delays;
Thy fame has spread wherever bat and ball
   Ring with their joyous clatter o'er the field.
On this thy birthday may no shadow fall
   And may it still a further hundred yield;
Thou art the centre of a million eyes
   Who love one summer game and sunny skies.

To commemorate Grace's jubilee

The Man and His Times

W. G. Grace

Horace G. Hutchinson

It used to be said, in the Eighties, that the best known man in England was the then Prince of Wales, later King Edward VII, and the second best known, W. G. Grace. I do not think the statement was exact. It might serve for London, where the heir to the throne was a familiar figure, but taking all the country over, towns and villages alike, I believe that the royal personage would not have been recognized, in spite of all the picture papers, nearly so readily and generally as 'W.G.'.

Of course 'W.G.' had an immense advantage, if it be an advantage to be thus recognized by the multitude, in his singularly recognizable figure – you could not forget him if you once had seen him. He was immense, both in height and bulk, taller in reality than he looked just because the bulk disguised the height. And then he had that big red face, and that big black beard. He would serve quite well for the figure of the ogre in a child's picture book – a very kindly ogre withal.

I heard two in a Club – the sort of place where you do hear pernicious nonsense – debating who had served the better of his country, who had given more delight in his generation, 'W.G.' or 'W.E.G.' Is it necessary to remind a modern audience that the latter were the initials of Mr. Gladstone? Of course the debate was futile: it is as vain as the assertion we have seen that Pitt was a greater man than Shakespeare. The two 'greatnesses' are not comparable, in the one case more than in the other: there is no common standard of measurement. One of my men in the

Club said, 'Go to the Reform – you will there hear that Gladstone is the greatest man the world has ever known, that Disraeli is the most pernicious. Go into the Carlton, there they will tell you that Disraeli is the great man of the world and that Gladstone is everything that is evil. The opinions balance each other, so that the sum total is zero to the credit of either. But go into any Club that you please, along St. James's Street and Piccadilly and Pall Mall, ask them about "W.G.", and every one of them will tell you the same story about him, that they are grateful for his existence, that he is a real benefactor, that he has given joy to thousands.'

That at least is true, and on that count we may rank 'W.G.' with the *prima donna* and the great actor. He was an actor, the finest we have ever had, on the twenty-two yard stick between the wickets – tragic, for the bowler and the side opposed to him, yet with an element of comedy always about him. You never hear any one speak of 'W.G.' even now without a smile of amusement curling up the lip both of speaker and listener. He was both to be laughed at and to be laughed with; but perhaps you had better do the former, at all events, with discretion. He was too big a man to be trifled with, and though he was kindly he was quite self-assertive. Sometimes they said that he was inclined to be rather too assertive on his rights, if not of a shade more than his strict rights, in the cricket field, but we have to remember that all that side of games, even of our greatest game, is governed by tradition, and that the tradition in which 'W.G.' and his brothers had been reared in Gloucestershire and the West was not precisely the same as that which prevails at Eton and Oxford, or Harrow and Cambridge, and so on. There was just a little of the 'win, tie, or wrangle' business about the game in the provinces, especially perhaps in the West, and it was all considered perfectly fair business, and 'all in the game', so to say. 'W.G.' really was not unsportsmanlike in insistence on points about which an Eton or Oxford captain, let us say, would not have insisted, because it was only part of the custom of his county and of the game as he knew it to be thus insistent; and he would not have resented at all a like insistence on the part of another. In fact I am not quite sure that he would not have thought another rather a fool if he did not insist . . .

How did it happen? How was it that, in a game which we all play, there should arise this one man so masterfully better than all his fellows? That is a question to which it is not likely we shall ever find an answer. One thing is quite sure, that it is a question which 'W.G.' could not have answered. Never was there a man less prone to theorize. The practice of the game was good enough for him. 'What's the best thing to do, "W.G."?' someone asked him, 'with those tricky balls of ——?' (I forget the bowler. It does not matter.) 'I should say,' was the answer, 'put the bat against the ball.' It is very sound advice, no doubt; whether it went far enough to be very helpful is another matter.

'Have you read Fry's book?' someone asked him. 'No,' he said, 'I am afraid to read it. I was afraid if I was to read it that Charles would bowl me out while I was trying to recollect what to do with a long-hop.'

I remember poor Alfred Lyttelton telling a story of 'W.G.' at a cricket dinner. Alfred, always most generous of opponents, was keeping wicket; 'W.G.' batting. 'Wait a moment, "W.G." ', he said, 'there are some fellows moving in the pavilion behind the bowler's arm.'

'Never mind, Alfred; never mind,' was the answer. 'I don't mind what they're doing in the pavilion; I keep my eye on the ball.' That is a story that some fussy batsmen might do well to lay to heart.

'How did it happen?' Lately a *Memorial Biography* of this greatest of cricketers has been published containing a thousand and one good stories about him from many pens. I am not sure, but I do not think that this, brought to my recollection by this phrase which I thoughtlessly wrote, is told there. It was on the voyage out to Australia, and amateur theatricals were among the pastimes of those weeks of leisure. 'W.G.,' who was not a practised actor, was cast for a part in which he had to say 'How did it occur?' He always did pretty well in the rehearsals until he came to this sentence, which he invariably paraphrased, 'How did it happen?'

'Well,' he said, when the stage manager corrected him. 'It means the same, don't it?'

And so it does – only, unfortunately, the sentence next to follow was 'It was not a cur; it was a very well-bred dog.' I hope I hurt no feelings by the suggestion that it was not exactly a very high-class drama.

So the man with his 'cur', but sadly at a loss for his 'cue', expostulated bitterly after being thus left *en l'air* in the third rehearsal running. 'Ah, well,' said 'W.G.', 'I'll do it all right on the night when it comes to the match; this is only practice at the nets.' 'I bet you don't "W.G." ', called out Briggs. And 'Done with you' was the response.

On the great night, as the drama worked up to the point of 'W.G.'s' speech, all attention was concentrated in the interest of hearing whether he would deliver it correctly, and how the unfortunate man with the cur would follow him. To the gratification of the audience and the relief of his fellow-player he delivered the speech with perfect exactness, but followed it up with the pronouncement, not found in the book of the play, and not at all to the assistance of the next speaker – 'and that's half a crown to me, Johnny Briggs!'

There were those who said that he ought to be rated as a professional, and of course we all knew that he took money for playing over and above the amount of his expenses by way of reimbursement for the fees he might otherwise have been earning in his profession. But, after all, he could not have played had he not done so; and if he had become a professional, the Gents *v.* Players matches of his time, and how long a time it was we know, would have had little interest. There would have been but one side 'in it'. With the professionals he was always popular; and he would travel long distances to play in a match in which one or other of them was taking his 'benefit' – to the certain enhancement of the gate-money.

In the evening of that life which seemed to most of us much longer than it really was, because he had come so early before the public, it must surely have been gratifying to him to reflect that in the playing of the game which he loved and in which he was the acknowledged master he had given such great pleasure to many millions.

PORTRAITS OF THE EIGHTIES, *T. Fisher Unwin Ltd., 1920*

William Gilbert Grace, 1848–1915

NEVILLE CARDUS

AMONGST the eminent Victorians was W. G. Grace; he enjoyed the proper authority. The nation called him the G.O.M., and, like another monument called the same, he looked the part. There is a lot in 'appearance' if the crowd is to give full respect and worship. W. G. Grace possessed physical size – and he was bewhiskered. I have seen faded photographs taken of Grace when he was under twenty years of age; the beard is already profuse and impressive. To catch the popular sense of dramatic fitness, Grace simply *had* to be big, for he stood for so much in the history of cricket at a time when hardly any other game challenged it as the national out-of-door sport and spectacle. Also there is another point which was to Grace's advantage in his character of a G.O.M.: he lived in a period which not only believed in great men but actually insisted on them and went about looking for them. And because there was no idea then of the trick of exploitation called nowadays publicity, a politician, actor, jockey, or a cricketer could remain at a romantic distance from the eyesight of the multitude: he did not get too familiar. Grace was a household possession, true, but only by reason of the performances he achieved day by day. Advertisement did not give him a spurious reputation and wear out belief in him by damnable iteration. Off the cricket field he was concealed in suggestive anonymity, and if people saw him in the streets, they turned round and gazed and gaped, and were pleased if they could feel that no mistake had been made.

Astonishing that by means of a game of bat and ball, a man should have been able to stamp his shape and spirit on the imagination of thousands. As I say, no rhetorical Press pointed out his prowess incessantly. Not long ago I had cause to look through the files of an old newspaper in search of some bygone fact of cricket. I found a match at Lord's in which W.G. scored 152 not out; the game was reported in very small type with no headlines but this – in tiny print:

Another Good Score by Dr. Grace

Grace got his renown during the years that did not know the literary persuasions of cricket writers who describe an innings by Hobbs in the rhetoric of a Macaulay; alone he conquered – with his bat and (this is certain) by his beard.

When I was a boy I lived in a family that did not interest itself in games. Yet often at breakfast W. G. Grace's name was mentioned. Everybody understood exactly who he was and what he signified in the diet of the day's news. From time to time, *Punch* used him as the subject for a cartoon; the Royal Family occasionally inquired after his health. When he was reported not out at Lord's at lunch, the London clubs emptied, and the road to St. John's Wood all afternoon was tinkling with the old happy noise of the hansom cab. Sometimes he would play, at the height of his frame, in a country cricket match in some village in the West of England. And from far and wide the folk would come, on foot, in carriages, and homely gigs . . .

I have always been amused that W. G. Grace became famous while the Victorians were endowing cricket with moral unction, changing the lusty game that Squire Osbaldeston knew into the most priggish of the lot, and stealing rigour, temper, and character from it. Cricket was approved at the private schools for the sons of gentlemen; the detestable phrase, 'It isn't cricket', was heard in the land. The game acquired a cant of its own, and you might well have asked why two umpires were necessary at all, and why the bowler ever appealed for leg-before-wicket. W.G. could not have contained his large humanity in any genteel pursuit; he was of more than ordinary human bulk, and therefore he had more than ordinary frailty. He exercised his wits, went about the job of winning matches with gusto.

'Did the old man ever cheat?' I once asked an honest Gloucestershire cricketer, who worshipped Grace.

'Bless you, sir, never on your life,' was the quite indignant answer. 'Cheat? No, sir, don't you ever believe it – he were too clever for that.'

When Grace and Gloucestershire met Hornby and Lancashire, there was sport indeed. Grace had a habit of moving a fieldsman surreptitiously from the slips to fine leg, while the batsman was concentrating his vision on the next ball. Once on a time at Old Trafford, A. N. Hornby decided to hoist Grace with his own petard. So, even as Grace was standing with his left toe up from the ground, getting ready for a stroke while the bowler was running to the wicket – at that very moment A. N. Hornby quietly signalled to first slip, who on tiptoe moved towards the leg side behind Grace's back. But he was not half-way there before W.G.'s high-pitched voice cried out: 'I can see what you're doin'; I can see what you're at!'

If a man is going to give his whole life to a game, let him play it like a *full* man, with no half-measures and no repressions. Cricket was a battle of wits with Grace, first and last. His enormous technique was saved from mechanical chilliness because he never practised it without some artful end in view; he larded the green earth wherever he played; he dropped juicy flavours of sport; he loved an advantage, and hated to be beaten.

In his long career, which lasted from 1863 to 1908, he scored more than 54,000 runs and took 2,864 wickets.* I write down these statistics here to give some slight idea of his mastery over the two main technical departments of cricket. But one of the purposes of my essay has really no use for records, which mean nothing to folk who are not cricketers. I am trying to get Grace into the Victorian scene, to see him as a Representative Man, and also to see him in relation to the crowd that invented his legend. 'Was he a fraud?' a young man at Oxford asked me not long ago. 'I fancy there is a bit of the fraud in all the Victorians.'

The question was, on the face of it, senseless: no charlatan can be a master and forge a lasting technique. There would have been no Hobbs if Grace had not extended the machinery of batsmanship and achieved a revolution in bowling, by his great synthesis of offensive and defensive stroke-play.

The hint of the triumphant charlatan which comes to us when we read of Grace (just as the same hint comes to us when we read of Gladstone and Irving) arises from a habit of mind supposed to be peculiar to the Victorians. They rather lacked flippancy, and for that reason they appear to this flippant generation to have blown out fulsomely all the objects of their admiration; they seized on the day's heroes, and invested them with the significance of a whole tradition. In an epoch of prosperity, when the idea of material expansion was worshipped for its own sake, even the vast runs made on a cricket field by W. G. Grace seemed symbolical; his perpetual increase of authority and performance suited a current love and respect for size and pros-

*See Philip Bailey, p. 154.

perity. W.G. became an Institution in a day of Institutions, all of which, like the Albert Memorial, had to be impressive by sheer bulk. W.G. himself, of course, did not know what he stood for in the national consciousness: he was content to be a cricketer. He shared none of the contemporary modern habit of self-exposition.

To-day, even though we pretend to possess a humorous sense of proportion, all sorts of small persons regard themselves much too seriously, and are ready to submit to an 'interpretation', psychological or scientific. I expect any moment a treatise by Bradman on 'The Theory and Economy of Batsmanship'. And I would not be surprised to hear, any Sunday evening, an address broadcast from St. Martin's by Jack Hobbs on 'The Cricketer as an Ethical Influence', with some moving metaphors about 'The Great Umpire' and 'Playing the Game'. W. G. Grace never lapsed into solemnity about himself . . . Frequently I wonder whether the 'Victorian age' has not been a consequence of the modern tendency to write 'studies' of everything; and to turn irony against itself by too close a search for significant overtones. Grace, I am sure, would be the last person in the world to regard himself a theme for such a 'study' as I am attempting now; I can see his great ghost stroking the immortal beard, and saying: 'Get on with the game.' It will be as well for me to do so; let me keep myself henceforth to the man's cricket; there's a deal to be said on behalf of it.

To be first in the field in any activity is a good thing: there's so much room in the beginning; the earth is virgin, and admiration is eager and sensitive. If a Grace were born to-day, what would there be in cricket left for him to do? – and a man cannot express an original nature by moving along worn tracks, emulating and not creating. When Grace began to stamp his personality on English sport, cricket was scarcely established, save as a rough-and-ready pastime on the village green. The technical elements of the game had yet to be gathered together; the counties had to be organized. A spectacular interest was wanting to attract the crowds; and the money was required to make a national game. W.G. came forward, at the ripe moment; the technique of cricket stood ready for expansion and masterly summary; the period was also ready for a game which everybody could watch, the gentry as well as the increasing population of town workers. Grace's skill as a batsman may be said to have orchestrated the simple folk-song of the game; his personality placed it on the country's stage.

He came from out of the West Country, and though in time his empire stretched from Lord's to Melbourne, never did he forget the open air of Gloucestershire, and the flavours of his birthplace. In an orchard at the dawning of June days, he learned his cricket; yet in his prime, at the age of forty-seven, he was still waking every summer morning fresh as a lad, eager for a match. If he knew that the other side were about to give a trial to a new bowler of awe-inspiring reputation, Grace would get up all the earlier, make haste to the field, and take a glance at the latest demon.

Once it happened that the Australians brought to England a bowler of unknown witchery; Grace straightway went to their captain, W. L. Murdoch, and he said: 'And so you've found a good bowler, eh? What does he do with the ball? Is he a fast 'un, or slow?'

'Ah,' was the sinister reply, 'he mixes 'em.'

'Very well, then,' answered W.G., 'I'll have a look at him this afternoon; I'll have a look at him.' And that afternoon he went in first with some old professional, whom we'll call Harry.

W.G. played a few overs from the new bowler most warily; the devil might have been in every ball, so carefully did Grace keep his bat down, and so suspiciously did his eyes sharpen. After a short time he hit the new bowler for two fours and a three off successive balls. And while the two batsmen were passing one another up and down the pitch, Grace's voice cried out, in immense glee: 'Run up, Harry, run up! We'll mix 'em for him; we'll mix 'em!' Is it any wonder that the man's vital character made cricket seem part of the English way of life in summer-time, lusty and manly, yet artful and humorous? A great company of 'originals' grew around the Old Man: Tom Emmett, A. N. Hornby, Crossland, Barlow, Johnny Briggs – scores of them, all men of ripe comedy, home-spun and fresh, each of them as vivid as characters on a page of Dickens or Surtees.

Cricket is not the best game *as* a game. There is more excitement in Rugby football; as much style and skill in tennis at Wimbledon; a swifter and more certain decision in a cup-tie. But cricket is without a rival amongst open-air pastimes for the exhibition of native characteristics in Englishmen. It is a leisurely game on the whole, and its slow movement enables the cricketers to display themselves. A lot of nonsense is talked about the 'team spirit' in cricket; but as a fact the greatest batsmen and bowlers and fieldsmen have been those who have stood out from the ruck and have taken charge of the situation in ways entirely their own. You could not merge into a drilled efficient mass the Johnsonian bulk of Grace, or the Figaro alacrity of a Macartney. In no other game than cricket does the result mean so little to true lovers of it. As the years pass by and cricketers become old and sit by the fireside talking of the past, they do not remember matches won or lost, or the scores piled up, or the technical excellences seen on a hundred fields of play. W. G. Grace put his heart into the game, and perhaps it is that which keeps cricket alive to this day, despite many changes and vicissitudes.

At the present time, nearly all the performances of W. G. Grace have been surpassed by cricketers here and there – some of whom will not be remembered a year after they have ceased playing the game. Hendren of Middlesex has scored more hundreds than W. G. Grace scored in his long career. Yet the fact of Grace's posterity remains to this moment: he is still the most widely known of all cricketers amongst folk who have seldom, if ever, seen a match. After all, he really did transcend the game; I have tried in this article not to treat him with less proportion than he would have treated himself. But I cannot, and nobody possibly could, contain the stature of the man within the scope of bat and ball. Nobody thinks of Grace in terms of the statistics recorded of his skill; like Dr. Johnson, he endures not by reason of his works but by reason of his circumferential humanity. I always thing of him as the great enjoyer of life who, after he had batted and bowled and fielded throughout the whole three days of a match between Gloucestershire and Yorkshire, was at the end of the third afternoon seen running uphill from the gound, carrying his bag, in haste for the train to London – running with a crowd of cheering little boys after him, and his whiskers blowing out sideways in the breeze.

THE GREAT VICTORIANS, *Nicholson & Watson, 1932*

The Age of Grace, 1864–1893

ROWLAND BOWEN

MANY of Grace's achievements would be rated extremely good by our standards – or rather not by our standards today which are poor, but by our knowledge of what has recently passed. By the standards of his day they were *phenomenal*: nothing like them had ever been done before, nothing like them had ever been publicized before. They were so far above the normal standards of good batsmen and good bowlers of the time when he came upon the scene as to set quite new standards, and it was *up* to his standards that cricket gradually rose during this entire period, so that by the end even some of Grace's records were being beaten or closely chased. But at the start, or in the middle of the period, there was no one who looked like doing so on the batting side: on the bowling, yes, because he made his batting his first aim. He was a very fine medium pace bowler, but something had to give if the man himself was not to. In a series of erudite and fascinating articles in *The Cricketer* in 1938 and 1939, the statistician George H. Wood (a Fellow of the Royal Statistical Society, elected as a result of a paper sent to it when he was in his middle teens) showed conclusively that W. G. Grace was far and away the finest all-rounder of English cricketers in the sixty years of cricket which was the subject of his survey. In that survey he attempted to quantify the effect of various changes in the laws, conduct and general appurtenances of the game on scoring and wicket-taking, and did so without any serious challenge: thus though his results now need to be added to, it is unlikely that any other English player has been found in the last twenty-five years, or will be found in the next thirty years, to challenge W.G.'s supremacy and it is not easy to think of any overseas player of any period who could have done so. Grace has been described as the first batsman to combine forward play with back play, but he had been preceded in this by Pilch whose example had had no permanent effect. Grace's did: no longer did batsmen confine themselves to one group of strokes, though there have always been those who have shown themselves stronger in one group, even in one stroke, than in the others. Grace made batting literally an all-round performance. Not only that: he revelled in hitting fast bowling, which is cricket as it should be played, and this was very definitely an example for others, since he showed that it could be done. He developed no one special stroke by which he became famous – he used them all, pragmatically as the occasion demanded. No one ever accused him of being a graceful bat to watch (no pun intended!) and if he had style it was that of the technician rather than of the artist. Artistry was to come later: perhaps, indeed, artistry could not come until the technical foundations had been safely laid.

This was why it is the age of Grace. But for Grace, it is unbelievable that the standards achieved by the Golden Age would have been thought of until, maybe, Bradman came along. He dominated the game, and any match in which he played: only Bradman appeared to dominate quantitatively in this way, but qualitatively, the difference was great. In fact Bradman did not do much that had not been done by one or other of his contemporaries. Grace did. Bradman had superb reflexes, but he did not possess the powerful physique that W.G. had: and with W.G. it was not just superb reflexes for he showed that what he did, anyone else could do, given application and perseverance and the massive physique to withstand punishment. But this last was not what Bradman could show. Yet . . . there had been another. Fuller Pilch had dominated the scene in his day in just such a way as Grace: statistically, the parallels between his performance and those of Grace are remarkably numerous: but Pilch does not stand out in history as does Grace because Pilch came on the scene at a period of very much lower scoring than before. He was seen in his own time as a wonderful cricketer: he never had the adulation which the populace bestowed on Grace.

Grace is important for another reason: it was not merely the first-class game which was dominated by him – he showed the way for all cricketers, and it is interesting and instructive to see how many records went by the board in minor cricket once he had shown what could be done. One question remains open: was all this because of Grace, or was it because of over-arm bowling? Or was it a little of each, over-arm being, in some respects easier to play (round-arm deliveries being so often wide of the wicket), if in others not so easy. The ball, being much straighter, had to be played, and Grace demonstrated that anyone, with talent, could play it, even if they could not achieve the summits of his own performance. It is very doubtful if any other great cricketer has ever influenced the game at all levels in the way that Grace did. It is even more doubtful if anyone ever will, or indeed if the conditions exist or can exist where anyone could: Grace's effort was a once-for-all one.

There was something else special about W.G. By the accident of his time, he became the first 'folk-hero' in modern times in England. There had been celebrated cricketers for over two hundred years from (and no doubt before) William Bedle down to Grace's own time. For the best part of a hundred and fifty years there had been great occasions when crowds of ten thousand, and later of twenty thousand and more, had gathered – formidable figures in view of the population totals and the difficulties of travel in horse-drawn days. But now, at the start of the modern era of cricket[1] there came this great man not yet heavily bearded and prefiguring Jove himself, with his fantastic performances. These performances were known throughout the country if not by the same evening then by the following morning – known to all in a far greater population (and one still increasing rapidly) than that which knew any of his predecessors. If he wished, the ordinary man could come up from almost any part of the country speedily and cheaply to see Grace play the next day. And if he could not make the journey, he might still see Grace, for Grace did not confine his cricket to London, nor to Bristol either, but toured with his team to all parts.

The late Monsignor Ronald Knox suggested in an amusingly fanciful essay that W. G. Grace and W. E. Gladstone were one and the same man: it could be argued that Grace travelled more widely and more energetically than the Grand Old Man of Liberal politics. He took his own masterful play to the people wherever they were: in first-class cricket his run total is well over 50,000 and the runs he made in minor cricket brought the known total to a few hundred short of six figures and it is reasonably certain that, taking into account games where his score is unknown, he achieved that colossal figure, approached by no other batsman at any time. He was 'The Champion' and people thronged to see him in all his majesty of frame and cricket ability.

The dispossessed proletariat in search of an identity had found, if not an identity in W.G., a god whom they could worship. If he had not arisen at the time he did it is very doubtful if he would have caught the right moment of history: someone else, most probably in some other walk of life, might have done so. Grace did not give cricket a new lease of life – it was anything but moribund – but he gave it, and especially the first-class game, a new dimension of life. If he had arisen later, his performances would have been no less wonderful statistically but they might well not have turned him into a figure of myth and legend. Industrial England was in bad need of a hero: as Grace rose, the monarchy was withdrawing into privacy so that at the height of W.G.'s powers, there was no national figurehead. W.G. by his exploits became that figurehead and became a folk-hero, just as Pelé is in Brazilian football (in circumstances not vastly different from those of W.G., if one makes a few adjustments).

Let us then look at the scene of important cricket in the country. There had been one important development in the 1840s, about half-way through, and its effects lasted about half-way through the present period: the great touring Elevens, the All England XI of William Clarke, and the United All England XI set up in opposition. These teams, consisting of great players of the time, had toured the entire country. They were first and foremost money-making businesses, but they also spread knowledge of the game and intensified enthusiasm for it. Although these two teams effectively only lasted a few years into the period, others sprang up, the United North of England XI (with quite a short existence) and the United South of England XI, to which W.G. and others of the Grace family became attached and which late in its life confusingly changed its name to the United XI. They attracted less support and interest as the years went by, partly because of the great increase in county matches, but were finally killed because of the extensive tours undertaken by overseas teams – the first two Australian teams (excluding the Aborigines who indeed also toured widely in 1868), the first Canadians, and the two Parsi teams, all of whom followed a pattern similar to that of the great Elevens, and who must have been superficially at least, more interesting, and so far as the Australians were concerned, more attractive too.

It was this association of the Grace family with the United South of England XI which was at the bottom of the allegations that the Graces took fees for playing cricket, and it was this that led to the exclusion in due course of the youngest of them, G. F. Grace, from the Gentlemen *v.* Players match at Lord's: the M.C.C. dictum being that a gentleman ought not to make any profit from playing cricket. This was, of course, an impeccable description of an amateur and was carefully worded so as to allow an amateur to take expenses. W.G. undoubtedly did take expenses – he openly acknowledged the fact – but what was, and is, insufficiently realized is that he had to pay for a *locum tenens* to run his practice while he was away playing cricket. What is also insufficiently realized is that he treated many poor patients entirely free: this in a period when the National Health Service was undreamt of. On the other hand, it does seem that in his earlier years, as well, probably, as with the U.S.E.E., W.G. took fees: that he asked for them is certain. This was well before he qualified as a doctor, and it was not out of line with the behaviour of other celebrated amateur cricketers before him, and for a long way back, in one form or another. Shamateurism in the game has a long history, and for a time W.G. was most probably a shamateur: no doubt there was an element of hypocrisy over all this, but W.G. was not alone in it. That it should have caused any problems in the latter 1870s, for the first time apparently, tells us no more than that this was when Victorian righteousness first interfered with cricket. It had taken a long time: it was in that same decade that bookmakers were heard for the last time at Lord's, shouting the odds. It has often been thought that the gambling aspect of the game had vanished a generation or more before, apart from whatever may have gone on between private individuals. But this is not so, and it did not vanish from the Australian scene as quickly as all that . . .. Many people have been unable over the years to understand just what is supposed to be wrong about gambling: now, in a generation which sees more gambling than for many years, and in which cricket too is involved, previous attitudes must seem very strange.

CRICKET: A HISTORY OF ITS GROWTH AND DEVELOPMENT,
Eyre and Spottiswoode, 1970

---

[1] It was a modern era in so many other ways: the rise of Grace only just preceded that of Gilbert and Sullivan, yet their political and social satire is wholly comprehensible even to the young among us (though teenagers are beginning to find it difficult). Political and social satire of *two* hundred years ago was no longer comprehensible to any but the historically well-educated among Grace and his contemporaries.

> IT WAS a gusty morning when a fast ball eluded W.G.'s bat and snicked a bail which fell to the ground. 'Windy day today, umpire,' remarked Grace replacing the bail. 'Make sure it doesn't blow your cap off on the way back to the pavilion,' was the umpire's reply.

Closing of an Epoch

E. W. SWANTON

It is fifty years to within a few days since W. G. Grace played for the last time in a Test match. Captain C. B. Fry has told exactly the manner of his going out: how he was late for the Selection Committee meeting that was to choose the team for the Second Test match of 1899: how, on his arrival, the Doctor, who was in the chair, put to him the point-blank question, 'Should Archie play at Lord's?': and how thus, unknowingly, he gave the decisive opinion which involved the great man himself standing down. Few eminent figures have found it easy to leave the stage, and we know that W.G. did not do so without a pang, but that he felt in his heart that the decision was the proper one.

The crowd at Trent Bridge, perhaps irked at England's rather moderate showing – they did not achieve their draw with much to spare – had been critical of his fielding, and to be barracked was an experience he neither understood nor appreciated. He was too slow now, too slow and too heavy, and perhaps, at fifty, his eye was not quite quick enough to cope with Ernest Jones. This, by the way, was W.G.'s last year with Gloucestershire, too, before the unfortunate misunderstandings that caused him to leave the West Country, and to launch his London County project. Thus, it could be said, we celebrate now the anniversary of a landmark in the county sense, for the Graces made Gloucestershire, and Gloucestershire were among the sponsors and founders of the County Championship.

But 1899 was the beginning and end of an era in several senses. It was the first year in which the Tests, instead of being the concern and responsibility of the various County clubs on whose grounds they took place, were brought under the management of the newly-formed Board of Control. Again, it was the first year in which their number was increased to five. The googly, too, with its revolutionary effect on the technique of batsmanship, was only a year or two ahead. It was the closing both of a century, and of one of the cricket ages.

I hardly think the average modern enthusiast can conjure any closely-detailed design of the cricket of fifty years ago. He knows from the photographs and the prints what the players looked like, he may have seen the short simple skeleton pads, the fashionable batting-gloves of the period, the caps with short peaks, and so on. He can imagine, perhaps, from the pictures the actions of some of the bowlers: of Tom Richardson, for instance, with his bounding, swinging run-up, and the dainty, slanting approach of Colin Blythe. But what of the batting? I confess that my own imagination, at least, is not equal to any clear impression of how W.G. went through the motions of batsmanship, or J. T. Tyldesley, or Victor Trumper.

In a more general picture certain features seem fairly well established. If an early film showing the action of a match could be brought to light I suppose the first thing that would strike the modern eye would be the direction of the bowling and the more formal disposition of the fielders. The faster bowlers, especially, kept their attack going at the off-stump or outside, and mid-on and square-leg had no assistance in guarding the on-side. Off-side play was the thing, though there were, of course, famous exponents of the various leg-hits, from Charles Fry downwards, and no one presumably bowled to 'Ranji' without a long leg. The leg-break, too, was coming into fashion, developed by C. L. Townsend, and practised, at its best, by Len Braund.

The off-theory itself, incidentally, was of no great antiquity. Mr. Altham records how, according to W.G., a Gloucestershire amateur, R. F. Miles, who bowled slow left-arm with no particular skill, threw up an innocent-looking barrage of wide half-volleys to Surrey one fine day on the Oval wicket with notable effect. The theory, apparently, extended gradually to the right-arm bowlers, causing, it may be added, much slow play, particularly on the part of the northern professionals.

It is a common cricket weakness to eulogize the past, and perhaps difficult, in these days of in-swingers and leg-slips, not to sigh for the old off-side play. But a conscientious comparison with fifty years ago must note that period as the one of pluperfect pitches, when marl and liquid manure were applied with more liberality than discretion, and the bowler's lot was harder than at any time in history. Within two years of W.G.'s last Test came Alfred Lyttelton's famous proposal to amend the law of l.b.w., the proposal that won the day at a full meeting of M.C.C., but failed to obtain the two-thirds majority needed to change the *status quo*.

As to what W.G. would think of modern cricket, a great deal might be hazarded, particularly by those who knew him and his generation. No doubt many things would appeal to him; the general skill of the wicket-keepers, which by all credible account exceeds those of the 'nineties, the scientific placing of the field, and, of course, the complicated art of the googly. How W.G. would, himself, have enjoyed ensnaring his victims with the one that went the other way!

Equally surely, some things would have mystified him; chiefly, I think, the decline of length in bowling, with all the inevitable consequences of that defection, which has so lowered the batsman's art. The cricket of 1899 was more formal and stereotyped, less flexible and ingenious. There was certainly a more implicit adherence to first principles, both in batting and bowling. More attractive? As to that, there are many whose views are worth very much more than mine.

'A CRICKETERS NOTEBOOK', *The Field, June, 1949*

Play on a Higher Plain

KENNETH GREGORY

THIS is a happy note on which to end, or would be but for shrill mutterings on Mount Olympus.

'Can't have it! Shan't have it! Won't have it!'

Before me stands a massive figure, hand plucking at beard.

'Look here, young feller.'

I rise, bow, and trust he is permitted to bat and bowl at both ends.

'I'm captain! The other day I took my cleaver and hit a golf ball off the summit, went two miles. There're bottles down wells all over Olympus. Just played against XXII of Hades. Ever heard of Attila? plays with a cross-bat like brother Edward. Got him caught at deep square-leg, my "bread and butter ball".'

I murmur congratulations.

'BOWLS! Who was responsible for the first bowls match between England and Scotland?'

'You, Doctor.'

'Who captained England?'

'You, Doctor.'

'Whose rink was never beaten in six matches?'

'Yours, Doctor.'

'Don't want 'em to forget me down there.'

BARCLAYS WORLD OF CRICKET, *Collins, 1980*

> WHEN a small boy at Lord's demanded W.G.'s autograph, the latter remembered his face and said, 'But I gave you my autograph at Brighton a month ago.' The boy replied, 'I know, but I swopped you for Dan Leno and a couple of bishops.'

APPENDIX:

STATISTICAL SURVEY

Career Highlights until 1895

ARTHUR J. WARING

THE first mention in the London Press of Mr. W. G. GRACE as a cricketer we find in *Bell's Life* of July 26th, 1857, when he played in a match at Rodway Hill for West Gloucestershire against Bedminster, he being at the time nine years old. His name was last on the list of batsmen, and he scored three runs not out. He played in one other match, and scored one run in the two innings; he also effected one catch in the field. In 1858 his name appears four times, and the result of four innings was two runs only; but in all the games thus far played in, it will be seen he was on the winning side. The result of three matches in 1859 was four runs for four innings, but in 1860 he certainly gave the first taste of his quality, for in a match against Clifton, a well-known club even in those days, he scored fifty-one, and his average for the season was 20.2. Very promising, indeed; for it must be remembered he was but twelve years of age, and the matches were all against recognized clubs, and were not school games. In 1861 his name appears for the first time as a bowler, by the capture of one wicket. Beyond noticing the increased number of matches played in, there is nothing to record further in this or the following year. But thus early his value as an all-round cricketer seems to have been quite discovered, and in 1863 we find him playing no less than twenty matches, the first being against an All England eleven at Bath, where he was *successful* in securing a 'pair of spectacles'. His highest innings was eighty-six, and as a bowler he secured fifty-six wickets, fifteen being credited to him in the match against Clifton College. In 1864 his name was included in an All England eleven playing against eighteen of Lansdown, and later in the year he was considered good enough to find a place in the tour of the South Wales Club. Right well did he justify this selection, for in the match at Brighton against Sussex he scored his first three-figure innings of 170. He also made his bow to a London audience, playing in matches at both Lord's and the Oval, and for the first time the full analysis of his bowling is given. It must be also recorded that he bowled his first no-ball and four wides. 1865 is a memorable year, for his fame had now become so well established that we find him playing at Lord's and the Oval, for the Gentlemen *v*. The Players. Though the coveted century was not reached, he played two innings of over eighty, and of the fifteen matches contested ten were won, five being single innings victories. In the Gentlemen of the South *v*. The Players of the South match, at the Oval, he took thirteen wickets for seventy-four runs. 1866 was a very noteworthy year. Playing for England against Surrey, at the Oval, he scored his first innings of over 200 – viz., 224 not out, this being the highest individual score ever made at the Oval up to date [1896]. Surrey made 99 and 126, *or one more run in their two innings* than Mr. Grace's score. In the *History of a Hundred Centuries*, Mr. Grace observes that 'on the last day of this match I was allowed to go away before the game was over, to run in the quarter-mile hurdle race at the Crystal Palace, which race, by-the-way, I won'. He scored another three-figure innings of 171, also at the Oval, and was again not out. In the course of this match he was presented with a bat to commemorate his 224 innings, and, having broken his old bat, continued his innings with the new one, and with it scored two sixes, run out, in rapid succession. During the West Glo'ster tour, in September, he did some excellent bowling performances, obtaining forty-eight wickets in the three matches against the twenty-two's of Ross, Monmouth, and Hereford. In the first two names the brothers E.M. and W.G. took all the wickets between them. 1867 is only noticeable for the few times he appeared in the cricket field. Of the seven matches played in, six were won, and one drawn.

In 1868 his name, for the first time, is associated with the United South of England eleven, and in the first match played for them, against twenty-two of Cadoxton, he *'bagged a brace'*; but the century was passed on five occasions, once the 200 exceeded. At Canterbury, for South of the Thames *v*. North of the Thames, he topped the century in each innings, a feat that had only been once previously accomplished. In the South *v*. North match, at Lord's, finished in one day, he took eleven wickets for sixty-six runs, and, for the first time, scored over 1,000 runs in the season.

A memorable year is 1869, as he first figures as a member of the M.C.C., and in his initial match for the club, against Oxford University, scored 117; and again, later in the season, against Surrey, carried his bat through the innings for 138. The century was reached no less than nine times, and with a tremendous bound he nearly doubled his previous number of runs for a season. Attention must be drawn to the Gentlemen and Players match, at the Oval. The Players went in first, and scored 475. Messrs. W. G. Grace and B. B. Cooper opened the innings for the Gentlemen, and put on 283 runs for the first wicket (record up to this date [1896]); the innings realized 553 runs. The Players scored 108 runs for one wicket in their second innings, when the match was drawn. 1,136 runs were scored for twenty-one wickets. Mr. Yardley, in a footnote to this match in *The History of a Hundred Centuries*, remarks: 'The match began at twelve o'clock on Thursday. Personally I did not go to the wickets till four o'clock on Saturday afternoon.' As a bowler he was highly tried, and, for the first time, more than a hundred wickets fell to his bowling.

In the third match played in 1870, for Bedminster against Swindon, he failed to score in either innings, but in a full season's cricket on only one other occasion did he so fail, and his high reputation was fully maintained. In the second innings of the Gentlemen *v.* Players, at the Oval, he scored 215, this being the highest individual score ever made in this match up to that date; the total of the innings, 513, was also a record. Another great performance, in the same titled match, was at Lord's, when he 'scored 109 out of 187, the match ending, after a most exciting finish, in favour of the amateurs by four runs. The century was exceeded eight times during the season.

In 1871 his performances were again very remarkable. In the first six matches contested the century was passed four times. In the South *v.* North match, played at the Oval, he scored 268, the highest individual score ever made on the ground up to then; and at Brighton, in the Gentlemen *v.* Players match, he exceeded the second century by seventeen. During the course of this match the Sussex County Club presented him and Mr. G. F. Grace with bats for their brilliant batting, and to 'W.G.' was also presented a bat given by the Surrey Club, to commemorate his great innings of 268, the bat bearing this inscription on a gold plate: 'Presented to W. G. Grace, Esq., by the Surrey C.C., for his magnificent innings of 268 in the match, South *v.* North, at the Oval, August 2, 1871'. In addition to the above, the century was exceeded on eight other occasions.

In a leaderette in the *Pall Mall Gazette*, of June 14th, 1895, entitled 'W.G.,' by W. G. Grace, he speaks of this as being his best batting year; and though the 3,022 runs scored during the season is not his greatest aggregate, still the analysis yields the phenomenal average of 67·1 per innings, which is his best.

In 1872 the pace slackened considerably, greatly due, doubtless, to the wetness of the season. Reference to the table for this year will show some extraordinary low scoring, yet, in spite of this, the Champion was able to add seven centuries to his list. And it may be also noted that he left England for Canada before the season was over. As a cricket curiosity we give the bowling analysis of the M.C.C. v. Surrey match, at Lord's. Surrey's bowling, first innings:

	Overs	Runs	Wickets
Mycroft	9	5	4
Southerton	9	11	6

1873 was a very full year's cricket, forty-two matches being played, and, though nothing of a very sensational nature was done, a highly satisfactory average of all-round excellence was maintained. Reference must be made to the Gentlemen v. Players matches, three under this title being played this year. In the first, at Lord's, he scored 163; the Players' first innings was 78. In the second, at the Oval, 158; the Players' first innings totalled 106. At Prince's, he was out for 70, giving an average for the three matches of 130.3. It may be noticed that in the Lord's match his individual score was more than *double* that of the Players' first innings, and at the Oval nearly so. Another feature to be noticed is that he was eight times 'not out', and that for the first time his bowling was credited with over 200 wickets; also that the 57 catches made in the field is his record.

The season of 1874 was opened in splendid style with an innings of 259 for Thornbury v. Clifton, and, though nothing further phenomenal occurred, the year holds the record for the greatest number of centuries obtained – viz., eleven. It is also noticeable that every innings played was completed. Another feature is the number of successful matches, twenty-two being won (twelve single innings victories) out of thirty-seven contested. His bowling is also well worthy of comment, and a reference to the analysis will show some extraordinary performances. 171 catches were made off his bowling, and the average of 9.3 runs for 267 wickets taken, gives his best record, and shows how difficult and tricky must have been his deliveries.

1875 holds first place for the greatest number of matches, days, and innings played. A performance worthy of notice was made in Gentlemen v. Players match at Lord's. W.G. went in first with Mr. A. J. Webbe, and 203 runs were put on for the first wicket – a record for the ground. With the ball he was 'dead on the spot', and succeeded for the first time in capturing over 300 wickets, the 195 catches made from his bowling being a record.

Still more records have to be chronicled in 1876. In this year 'Our

Champion' scored *three thousand seven hundred and forty-one runs*, the greatest number ever made by him during a season, and topping his previous best by nearly 800. Other phenomenal performances to be noticed are his 400 not out against twenty-two of Grimsby – a record against a twenty-two (and only twice exceeded in cricket annals). At Canterbury, in the M.C.C. *v.* Kent match, he scored 344, made in six hours twenty minutes, *without giving a chance.* This was followed by 177 in the Glo'ster *v.* Notts. match, and in the next game, against Yorks., he carried his bat through the innings for 318, this being the highest score ever made in a county match up to this date. In these three consecutive innings 838 runs were scored, once not out, *yielding the extraordinary average of 419.5 runs per innings.*

1877 stands out more prominently as a batting than a bowling year, though, out of fifty-seven innings, only once did he fail to score. The second hundred was well passed on one occasion, and the century four other times. A very noticeable feature of this year is the number of successful contests, twenty-four victories being gained (a record as far as our tables are concerned), and only *twice was his side beaten.* In bowling, the following figures give some very striking results. In the South *v.* North match, at Lord's, he got eight wickets for thirty-six runs; in the Glo'ster *v.* Sussex match, at Hove, seven for forty-six; for Glo'ster *v.* Notts., at Trent Bridge, six for twenty-three; against Surrey, at Clifton, five for twenty-five; and in the return match, at Cheltenham, against Notts., seventeen for eighty-nine; *Out of the last seventeen balls bowled, he took seven wickets for no runs.* The year holds the record for the greatest number of wickets – viz., 338, of which 112 were clean bowled, this also being a record.

1878 shows a great drop in the run-getting department, and the century was only once passed. The year is memorable for the first visit of an Australian team, and their first match in London, at Lord's, against the M.C.C., was highly sensational. M.C.C. went in first, and scored thirty-three; the Colonials forty-one. M.C.C. were all out the second time for nineteen (Flowers eleven). The match was over in one day. The Australian bowling for the two innings, reads:

	Overs	Runs	Wickets
Spofforth	14.3	20	11
Boyle	21.1	17	8

Of W.G.'s bowling it is sufficient to note that in the Glo'ster *v.* Sussex match, at Hove, he took four wickets for thirteen runs, and in the return match six for thirteen, and that twenty-six wickets out of thirty-four fell to his share in the U.S.E. *v.* Eighteen of Essex match.

Only twenty-one matches were played in 1879, and figures consequently show a decrease all round. During the match, at Lord's, Over
Thirty v. Under Thirty, a testimonial consisting of a clock, ornaments,
and cheque amounting in all to the value of about £1,400, was presented
by Lord Fitzhardinge to Mr. W. G. Grace, in recognition of his abilities
as a cricketer. And a correspondent to the *Sportsman*, giving his batting
performances for the year, remarks: 'Mr. Grace's supremacy is not yet a
thing of the past.' The spirit of prophecy had evidently descended on
this gentleman.

In a quiet year's cricket, in 1880, the century was passed four times,
and a record established in the fact that, out of fifty-one innings played,
not once did he fail to score.

In 1881 the good average of fifty-five runs per innings may be noted,
and his 182 at Trent Bridge, in the Glo'ster v. Notts. match, was a record
for the ground. At Thornbury, on July 19th, the tables show that he
scored his hundredth century. In 1884 his fine batting against the
Australians is well worthy of comment, as one three occasions when
playing against them he exceeded the century. 1885 is remarkable for a
score of 221 not out, made in six hours twenty minutes, in the Glo'ster v.
Middlesex match, at Clifton, and for the centuries made against Surrey
and the Players. Leaving out the Somerset match (not a first-class
county then), the table shows the following figures: 104, 19, 221, 68, 174,
or 586 runs – twice not out – giving an average 195.3 runs per innings. It
may be also noticed that in the M.C.C. and Lancashire, and the Glo'ster
and Notts. matches, he was out l.b.w. on three consecutive occasions.

1886 shows the greatest number of runs scored off his bowling during
the season, and holds the record for the number of successful appeals
for l.b.w., twenty-one of the 140 wickets taken being obtained in this
manner.

1887 will be remembered for its glorious summer, and as a consequence we find a high aggregate of runs, in the Glo'ster v. Kent match at
Clifton. For the second time the century was reached in each innings,
the last ball but one bowled in the game giving him this distinction.
Against Yorks at Clifton he was only eight short in the first innings, and
scored 183 not out in the second. He carried his bat nine times, and fifty-
four innings resulted in the splendid average of 52.7.

In compiling his 216 against Sussex at Brighton in 1888 he was in the
whole of the first day for 188; and in the Glo'ster v. Yorks he for the third
time – and for the second year in succession – secured the century in
each innings. It will be noticed that on the three times this great feat was
accomplished his side has not won, once being beaten and on the other
occasions the matches were drawn. There is nothing to record in 1889,
except that he scored over a century in each of the matches against

Middlesex, carrying his bat for 127 in the second played at Clifton. 1890 and 1891 may be passed without any comment, and 1892 is only remarkable for the fact that for the *first time* since 1867 the century was not reached; but 1893 proved a good batting year, over 2,000 runs were scored during the season, and once the second century was passed. 1895 showed that, in spite of advancing years, his batting had lost but little, if any, of its brilliancy, and his aggregate of 2,467 runs for the *season is the highest since his record of 1876* – a most wonderful accomplishment for his thirty-ninth cricket year, and well worthy of the universal recognition that was made to him by his friends and admirers throughout the whole length and breadth of the civilized world. It is also pleasing to have another record to chronicle in this great year, for in the Glo'ster *v.* Kent match at Gravesend, after Kent had scored 470 in their first innings, he was the last man out on his side with 257, and going in first again in the second innings carried his bat for seventy-three when the match was won for Gloucester. He was therefore 'on view' in the field either batting or bowling from the first ball delivered in the game to the finish, the second century was passed once, and *the hundred on eight other occasions.*

'W.G.', OR THE CHAMPION'S CAREER, Alexander & Shepheard, 1896

W. G. Grace Revisited

PHILIP BAILEY

THE *traditional* figures for Grace were originally compiled by F. S. Ashley Cooper in 1896 and published in *Cricket* 1896 p. 470, 483 and 1897 p. 14 and 30, in a series of four articles. These however only dealt with batting performances. Ashley-Cooper noted: 'I have included MCC v Herts and MCC v Staffs, which although not really first-class, have always been reckoned in W.G.'s average for 1873' (in fact this is not strictly true, since Lillywhite's Annual for 1874 did not include these matches and gave: 28 inns 4 no 1,647 runs). Ashley-Cooper also failed to mention his own additions to 1872, which will be referred to later. In Wisden 1916, Ashley-Cooper printed basically the same figures again, though with minor amendments to 1865, 1866, 1874 and 177. These 1916 figures are still given in Wisden 1987, Playfair Cricket Annual 1987 and Frindall's *Wisden Book of Cricket Records* 1986 edition. There is an article by J. D. Coldham in *The Cricketer Quarterly*, Autumn 1981, which notes some of the variations in compilers' figures for Grace. The 1916 figures, which I shall use as a base for this article are:

Season	Inns	NO	Runs	100s	Runs Conc.	Wkts	OW
1865	8	1	189	0	268	20	
1866	13	2	581	2	434	31	
1867	6	1	154	0	292	39	
1868	13	2	625	3	686	48	1
1869	24	1	1,320	6	1,255	73	
1870	38	5	1,808	5	782	50	
1871	39	4	2,739	10	1,346	79	
1872	32	3	1,561	6	736	62	6
1873	38	8	2,139	7	1,307	101	5
1874	32	0	1,664	8	1,780	140	
1878	48	2	1,498	3	2,468	191	
1876	46	4	2,622	7	2,458	129	
1877	40	3	1,474	2	2,291	179	
1878	42	2	1,151	1	2,204	152	
1879	29	3	993	3	1,491	113	
1880	27	3	951	2	1,480	84	
1881	25	1	917	2	1,026	57	
1882	37	0	975	0	1,754	101	
1883	41	2	1,352	1	2,077	94	
1884	45	5	1,361	3	1,762	82	
1885	42	3	1,688	4	2,199	117	
1886	55	3	1,846	4	2,439	122	
1887	46	8	2,062	6	2,078	97	
1888	59	1	1,886	4	1,691	93	
1889	45	2	1,396	3	1,014	44	
1890	55	3	1,476	1	1,183	61	
1891	40	1	771	0	9 73	58	
1891/2	11	1	448	1	134	5	
1892	37	3	1,055	0	958	31	
1893	50	5	1,609	1	854	22	
1894	45	1	1,293	3	732	29	
1895	48	2	2,346	9	527	16	
1896	54	4	2,135	4	1,249	52	
1897	41	2	1,532	4	1,242	56	
1898	41	5	1,513	3	917	36	
1899	23	1	515	0	482	20	
1900	31	1	1,277	3	969	32	
1901	32	1	1,007	1	1,111	51	
1902	35	3	1,187	2	1,074	46	
1903	27	1	593	1	479	10	
1904	26	1	637	1	687	21	
1905	13	0	250	0	383	7	
1906	10	1	241	0	268	13	
1907	2	0	19	0	—	—	
1908	2	0	40	0	5	0	
TOTAL	1,493	105	54,896	126	51,545	2,864	12

In 1951 Roy Webber published the first edition of his *Playfair Cricket Record Book*, this first comprehensive 'modern' compilation resulted in many questions being raised, amongst which were the *traditional* Grace career figures. Webber made a detailed study of these and in an article in *Playfair Cricket Monthly* February 1961, he analysed the matches used by Ashley-Cooper in Wisden 1916, and then produced his own revised figures by excluding matches that he did not regard as first-class. After the 1873 season the Lillywhite annuals had printed a table of Grace's match-by-match figures for that summer and included some minor matches to enable Grace to reach 2,000 runs and 100 wickets. Ashley-Cooper had noticed this, but instead of deleting the minor matches, he added similar matches played in the 1872 season for the sake of consistency. These matches were MCC v Hertfordshire 1872 and 1873 (in fact Gentlemen of MCC in 1872 when 12-a-side played), MCC v Staffordshire 1873 (12-a-side), Amateur XI of England that toured Canada in 1872 v 15 Gentlemen of MCC (with Rylott) 1873, and, worst of all, two games played as fill-in games for one day only, between South and North in 1872 and 1873, because the original (first-class) match finished before the scheduled time (the matches were arranged for Thursday, Friday and Saturday, and much money would be lost if no play took place on the Saturday).

None of these games has any legitimate claim to first-class status and indeed in all the major contemporary cricket publications, only Grace's performances in the 1873 matches have ever been counted as first-class. Staffordshire and Hertfordshire (which teams have never played first-class cricket) played regular annual matches v MCC, which no-one has ever considered as first-class. A 'fill-up' game was quite a common feature when important matches finished early (because of the last day falling often on a Saturday) and none of these, apart from Grace in 1873, has ever been included in contemporary first-class averages. By their very nature they were basically one-innings a-side contests and purely 'exhibition' contests – in one such Grace actually batted with a broomstick, whilst the rest used bats.

In addition Webber excluded from Ashley-Cooper's figures matches played between Gloucestershire and Somerset, 1879 to 1885 and two matches by England XI v Kent XIII in 1878 and 1879, because Kent accepted odds.

Grace's performances in these matches were as follows:

1872	10/5	M CC v Staffordshire	0,75	5/37, 1/17
1872	27/7	South v North	1	6/?
1873	9/5	MCC v Hertfordshire	47, 26	7/19, 5/21
1873	19/7	MCC v Staffordshire	67	5/25, 7/50

1873	21/7	Amateur Tourists v XV MCC	152, 5	1/79, 1/8
1873	26/7	South v North	37*	5/?
1878	5/8	England v XIII of Kent	21, 14	4/72, 1/21
1879	4/8	England v XIII of Kent	3, 63*	5/38, 1/45
1879	11/8	Gloucs v Somerset	113	6/30, 2/47
1881	14/7	Gloucs v Somerset	80	1/45, 4/31
1881	18/8	Gloucs v Somerset	15, 30	3/53, 4/15
1882	13/7	Gloucs v Somerset	1	8/31, 2/53
1883	9/8	Gloucs v Somerset	40, 43	5/39, 5/67
1883	13/8	Gloucs v Somerset	75, 58	5/59, 6/95
1885	5/8	Gloucs v Somerset	16	0/49, 3/51
1885	27/8	Gloucs v Somerset	36, 22	5/60, 0/69

Webber also noted the following errors in scores published in *Scores & Biographies*:

1869 11/8 MCC v Kent(1) Grace conceded 60 not 122 (Green 41)

1873 5/6 Gentlemen of South v Players of North(2) Grace conceded 30 not 40 (Brice 32)

1873 14/8 Gloucs v Yorkshire(1) Grace conceded 46 not 48 (G.F. Grace 49, Lang 33)

Webber's article notes a 9 run discrepancy due to differences in scores between Wisden and S&B – the other three come in the Staffordshire match above where Wisden has 78 runs conceded and S&B has 75. He also notes an error in the compilation of the averages for 1889 where Grace conceded 1,019 (as per scores) not 1,014.

The following revised seasonal totals result:

Season	Inns	NO	Runs	100s	Runs Conc.	Wkts	OW
1869	24	1	1,320	6	1,193	73	
1872	29	3	1,485	6	682	56	
1873	32	7	1,805	6	1,093	75	
1878	40	2	1,116	1	2,111	147	
1879	26	2	814	2	1,331	99	
1881	22	1	792	2	882	45	
1882	36	0	974	0	1,670	91	
1883	37	2	1,136	1	1,817	73	
1885	39	3	1,614	4	1,970	109	
1889	45	2	1,396	3	1,019	44	
TOTAL	1,468	103	53,856	124	50,250	2,762	1

These revised totals (together with the traditional figures) appeared in Webber's *Playfair Book of Cricket Records* 1961 edition and Frindall's *Kaye Book of Cricket Records* in 1968.

When the Association of Cricket Statisticians was formed in 1973 the primary aims included publication of a complete list of first-class matches with corrections to existing published match scores and follow-ing on from these two objectives, an accurate set of career statistics and first-class records. The first stage to be completed was the publication of the British Isles match list in 1976, which had been the result of much research and some preliminary articles in the ACS Journal. All sub-sequent ACS publications have adhered to this list. The list concluded that whilst Webber was clearly correct to omit the minor matches in 1872 and 1873, some of his other exclusions were too drastic. Contemporary opinion regarded Somerset as first-class between 1882 and 1885, so only the 1879 and 1881 Gloucs. v Somerset matches should be excluded and not those for 1882, 1883(2) and 1885(2). The matches between MCC England and XIII of Kent in 1878 and 1879 were also found to be included as first-class in contemporary annuals and thus are included in the ACS list – they formed part of the Canterbury Festival Week which was one of the highlights of the cricket calendar. However one match Webber did not question has been omitted from the ACS list, because Gloucestershire did not rate as first-class in contemporary annuals until 1870:

1868	25/6	Gloucestershire v MCC	24,13	4/47, 1/?

The following revised seasonal totals result:

1868	11	2	588	3	639	44
1879	28	3	880	2	1,414	105
1878, 1882, 1883, 1885 as Ashley-Cooper's figures						
TOTAL	1,478	104	54,211	124	50,952	2,808

There remains the question of differing bowling analyses – from 1869 when Wisden first published analyses until 1878 (the last year covered by S&B) there are several matches each season where Wisden and Scores & Biographies give differing details, both of which balance. Ashley-Cooper and Webber (except where noted already above) use the S&B version in each case. Although it has not been possible to prove each case, the evidence when researching for the ACS County series and pre-1900 scores suggests that Wisden is more reliable and with one exception noted these figures appeared in the ACS pre-1900 match scorebooks. There are also several cases where the analyses in S&B do not balance and those in Wisden do, and also a few instances where research in County Scorebooks available (notably for Sussex) shows up further errors in published scores. In the lists that follow those correc-tions made since June 1981 Journal article are marked†. The total given in the Journal of 50932-2809 appeared in the 1981 edition of Frindall's Wisden Book of Cricket Records (and still appears in the 1986 edition in one place, presumably unintentionally!)

Wisden 1981 used figures of 50999-2809, but the traditional figures were reinstated in 1982, when an article by Michael Fordham appeared which sought to justify the change. The differences from the June 1981 Journal to Fordham's article are the 1866 bowling analysis discovery and Wisden/S&B differences in 1874. Since then further research has yielded the figures of 50982-2808 which appeared in the ACS *Who of Cricketers*.

The difference in total wickets is catered for by the following, yielding an unchanged total of 2808:

†1874 11/6 Gloucestershire v Sussex(1) 4 not 5, Hall b G. F. not W. G. Grace
1876 27/7 Gloucestershire v Notts.(2) 5 not 4, Padley c E. M. Grace b W. G. not G. F. Grace
(1874 total should as a result read 139 wkts, and 1876 130)

It should be noted that in the cases where wickets differ in analyses, Wisden has always been preferred by all major publications.

The list of corrections in S&B is as follows:
†1866 21/5 Gents of England v Oxford U(1) no analyses given in S&B
1866 25/6 Gentlemen v Players(2) 49 not 69
1867 8/7 Gentlemen v Players(1) 39 not 38
1869 15/7 MCC v Nottinghamshire(2) 61 not 63 (Marten 65, Hearne 60, Money 60, Sutton 15, Green 17)
1870 18/8 Gents of South v Gents of North(1) 89 not 90 (Strachan 58, Rutter 62)
1871 3/7 Gentlemen v Players(1) 16 not 15
1871 9/8 Gents of MCC v Kent(2) 77 not 79
1871 14/8 Gentlemen v Players(2) 52 not 51 (Appleby 63, Walker 9, Total 147)
1872 25/7 South v North(1) 74 not 78 (Lillywhite 48, Willsher 21)
1875 29/7 Gloucs. v Notts.(2) 26 not 20
1877 14/5 MCC v England(1) 27, not 26 (Morley 15, Pearson 16)

The list of corrections to runs conceded in Wisden:
1879 21/7 Over 30 v Under 30(1) 54 not 55 (Mycroft 21) and (2) 33 not 32 (Mycroft 18)
1881 13/6 Gloucestershire v Middx(2) 54 not 57

The list of cases where S&B analyses balance but Wisden version accepted:
1869 24/6 Gentlemen v Players(1) 60 not 59 (Buchanan 97) (2) 75 not 77 (Buchanan 86, Absolom 39)
1869 1/7 MCC v Surrey(2) 48 not 47 (Hearne 28)
1869 15/7 Gentlemen of South v Players of South(2) 12 not 13 (Walker 32)
1869 9/8 South v North(2) 29 not 30 (Southerton 74, Willsher 21, Silcock 17)
1870 23/6 MCC v Oxford U(2) 21 not 20 (Farrands 46)
1870 28/7 Gloucs. v Surrey(1) 35 not 32 (Miles 86, G. F. Grace 35)
1871 21/9 W. G. Grace's XI v Kent(1) 67 not 68 (H. Grace 37)
†1874 4/6 South v North(2) did not bowl (not 3) (G. F. Grace bowled)
†1874 20/7 Gentlemen of South v Players of North(2) 79 not 78 (Renny-Tailyour 9, Gilbert 33).

1875 7/6 Gloucs. v Surrey(1) 71 not 72 (Townsend 29, Miles 12)

1876 29/6 Gentlemen v Players(1) 103 not 104 (Hadow 45)

1876 6/7 Gentlemen v Players(1) 76 not 77 (Patterson 63)

1876 20/7 South v North(1) 55 not 54 (Townsend 82)

1877 28/6 Gentlemen v Players(2) 93 not 92 (Patterson 85, G. F. Grace 58, Strachan 46, Gilbert 38, Lucas 48, Walker 19)

1878 6/6 South v North(1) 73 not 70 (Southerton 45) and (2) 59 and 58 (Southerton 62)

Note: 1870 9/5 Right-handed v Left-handed S&B accepted 43 – Wisden has 44)

Other corrections where published analyses balance:

†1874 11/6 Gloucs. v Sussex(2) 61 not 82 (G. F. Grace 82 – O, M, R all interchanged)

†1887 30/5 Gloucs. v Sussex(2) 66 not 62 (Newnham 50)

†1889 10/6 Gloucs. v Sussex(1) 116 not 115 (Radcliffe 54, Roberts 75)

†1890 26/5 Gloucs. v Sussex(1) 70 not 71 (Roberts 87)

Finally there is one case where the analyses in Wisden are definitely correct (from the Essex scorebook)

1898 15/8 Gloucs. v Essex(2) 6 not 8 (Brown 8)

Ashley-Cooper had inverted Grace and Brown's bowling to agree with the averages published in Wisden, but the scores are correct and the averages in error.

The above corrections lead to the revised totals for runs conceded:

1866 483, 1867 293, 1869 1189, 1870 785, 1871 1345, 1872 678, 1874 1757, 1875 2473, 1876 2457, 1877 2293, 1878 2208 (2203 in ACS June 1981 Journal was a misprint), 1881 879, 1887 2082, 1889 1020, 1890 1182, 1898 915.

TOTAL 50982

To complete the picture a list follows of corrections to published scores in S&B and Wisden which were known by Ashley-Cooper and incorporated into his compilation:

1873 12/6 Gloucestershire v Sussex(2) Phillips st Bush b W. G. Grace not G. F. Grace. W. G. 4w, G. F. 4w

1876 27/7 Gloucestershire v Notts.(1) Selby lbw b W. G. Grace, not G. F. Grace, W. G. 1w, G. F. 3; (2) Barnes c J. A. Bush b G. F. Grace, not W. G. Grace; Shaw c Gilbert b G. F. Grace not W. G. Grace; Tye c E. M. Grace b G. F. Grace not W. G. Grace. W. G. 5w, G. F. 4

1878 25/7 Gloucestershire v Lancs.(2) Grace scored 58* not 57* (Midwinter 25)

1878 5/8 England v Kent(1) Jones b Shaw not c Ridley b W.G. Grace. Grace 4w, Shaw 3w

1880 2/8 Gloucestershire v Australians (2) Grace scored 3 not 5 (E. M. Grace 41, Midwinter 12, Townsend 1, G. F. Grace 10, Cranston 6, Gilbert 10, Moberley 8, Fairbanks 1*, Gribble 1, Bush 0. Extras 4, Total 97)

1885 11/6 Gloucestershire v Surrey (2) J. M. Read c Woof b Grace

1889 22/8 Gloucestershire v Middlesex (1) Grace conceded 32 not 33 (Roberts 37)

1889 29/8 Gentlemen v I. Zingari (2) Grace conceded 14 not 15 (Stoddart 41)

Final Summary of W.G.'s Perform-ances in Minor Matches 1857–1914

G. N. WESTON

Year	Runs	Wickets	Catches
1857	4	0	1
1858	17	0	1
1859	12	0	1
1860	87	0	3
1861	125	5	6
1862	302	22	11
1863	669	81	13
1864	1,260	161	13
1865	1,972	189	18
1866	1,583	198	19
1867	654	83	8
1868	1,200	96	8
1869	1,026	81	8
1870	1,452	98	32
1871	1,074	106	22
1872 (At Home)	441	32	22
(In Canada & U.S.A.)	567	76	22
1873	925	123	38
(18/3/74 – In Australia)	866	99	37
1874	1,187	130	23
1875	1,293	217	24
1876	1,268	88	26
1877	997	211	20
1878	658	184	20

1897 5/8 Gloucestershire v Middlesex (1) Grace conceded 30 not 31 (Townsend 17)

1897 27/5 Gloucestershire v Kent (2) Grace scored 56* not 55

1901 22/7 London County v Leicestershire (2) Grace did not bowl. (not 0/12; McGahey bowled)

Note: The batting correction in 1878 is the missing run in the June 1981 ACS Journal compilation.

The final figures for W. G. Grace are therefore as given in the ACS Who's Who: 1,478 innings; 104 not outs; 54,211 runs; 124 100s; 50,982 runs conc; 2,808 wkts.

THE CRICKET STATISTICIAN, summer 1987

1879	35	19	0
1880	1,150	133	7
1881	1,360	172	12
1882	1,404	175	9
1883	1,218	119	5
1884	703	56	4
1885	494	57	2
1886	233	31	3
1887	409	45	7
1888	197	34	6
1889	978	96	15
1890	218	20	6
1891	530	49	5
1891/92 (Australian trip)	555	50	35
1892	53	17	0
1893	654	36	12
1894	613	77	10
1895	239	5	6
1896	295	17	2
1897	343	20	7
1898	272	13	3
1899	1,459	82	10
1900	1,398	130	8
1901	2,011	111	14
1902	1,458	115	7
1903	1,255	59	9
1904	944	111	8
1905	1,118	123	7
1906	869	68	9
1907	1,033	104	12
1908	687	124	6
1909	41	1	0
1910	418	21	5
1911	369	30	4
1912	149	3	3
1913	247	6	3
1914	205	4	0
TOTAL	45,283	4,578	656

Stumpings

Minor Matches
1863   3 (1 Extra)
Now a total of 52 in Minor Matches and 55 in *All* Matches

W. G. GRACE, THE GREAT CRICKETER,
Completed Supplement Typescript, Ltd Edn 4, 1980